REDEEM
THE STORY

A Call to Let God
Rewrite Your Story

Aaron Hall

HallMedia.org

Here's what others are saying...

"Your daily experiences mark and make your story what it is. But can your story be altered? In his new book, *Redeem the Story*, Aaron Joseph Hall explains how a personal relationship with Jesus Christ changes your story completely, immediately and eternally. Jesus causes old things to pass away and new things to come. He transforms you into a new creation and changes your story into a beautiful testimony of his love, mercy and grace. This book is filled with hope, a rare commodity these days, yet something we all need. I highly recommend this work."

Steve Gaines, PhD,
Senior Pastor, Bellevue Baptist Church,
Memphis, Tennessee

"Aaron Joseph Hall traces the thesis thread that runs through the treatise of truth, namely, redemption. Indeed, the Bible, when viewed from 30,000 feet up, reveals a narrative ark of hope. Its story shows that no trauma is too fatal to be redeemed. I'm grateful to have Aaron as a friend. So, develop richer, thicker grey matter in your prefrontal cortex, boost your brain intelligence, and enhance your spiritual deeps, by plunging into this book!"

Ben Courson,
Bestselling Author of Optimisfits,
BenCourson.com

"Aaron has a fresh perspective on the true role of redemption. Follow his easy writing style as he leads you in pursuit of your story of redemption. I have known Aaron for several years now and love his heart to reach a generation with the uncompromising message of redemption. He is a voice of righteousness in the midst of a darkened generation. His message of redemption and the uniqueness of each person possessing their own version of that glorious redemption is a fresh take on a much-needed subject."

Joel Stockstill,
Author of *Power of Daily Bible Reading*

"Aaron Joseph Hall is not only an amazing man of God, but a friend and talented author. His desire and heart to serve God and his people is unparalleled to any other I have met. His desire to write, preach, and disciple is inspiring. His heart for service to God's people goes above and beyond his call to duty. The most amazing part about all of this is he's so gifted and he will never claim a moment of the glory, but points it all back to our creator Christ. The more I have the opportunity to be around him the more I see how he's a prime example of what reckless obedience to following Jesus with all you have looks like. It's a pleasure and honor to know and work with him."

Etienne Doucet,
Youth Pastor,
Grace Bible Church in Sebring, FL

"Aaron Joseph Hall is passionate about his pursuit of the Lord, and a desire to reach the lost. His passion comes out as he shares his story of God's glory. It is obvious from the pages of *Redeem the Story* that Aaron draws from a deep well that comes from a steadily growing relationship with the Almighty!"

Pastor Cary McKee,
More 2 Life Ministries, Inc.

"Aaron Joseph Hall brings the redeeming work of God to the forefront of our lives through a combination of insightful Biblical Truth and Transparent personal experience. Where the power of God meets personal testimony, lives cannot help but be transformed!"

Pastor Tim Welborn,
Okeechobee, FL

"Knowing your story is one of the best tools that one has to share the gospel with anyone. But learning to craft it is a different story. To know and understand how one came to know Christ is very important not just for the believer but for those that come in contact with on a daily basis. I really like that Aaron starts out with the amazing stories of God's grace through scripture and how they used it to impact the nation of Israel and the world as we know it. Of all the tools that are out there in evangelism, know how to share your story is one that cannot be easily refuted or denied. I feel that this book will help many know that wither they came to know Jesus at age 5 at VBS, as a teenager, or through tragedy that they can effectively know how to tell others the Good News through their story.

"I would love to see this book published and in the hands of students and adults. Working with 100's of students and youth pastors on public school campuses this is the number one approach in reaching the lost. Students have amazing stories to share but just need to understand better the power behind it."

Jeff Stanford,
Regional Director First Priority of South Florida

Printed in the United States of America
First Print: January 2020, Second Print October 2025

ISBN 979-8-766-62261-6

Details in some anecdotes and stories have been changed to protect the identities of the persons involved.

Published by Hall Media (formerly Revive Press)
Okeechobee, Florida
Visit author website: HallMedia.org
Edited by Marcy Kompare
Sources Edited by Shayla Raquel, ShaylaRaquel.com
Publishing and Design Services: MartinPublishingServices.com

Dedicated to my wife, Sarah.

I love how God has intertwined our stories for His glory. Thank you for all you do! You have helped me with this project in more ways that I can say. Thanks, babe, for always being Jesus to me and others. You are a walking example of God's love and grace. This book wouldn't have happened without your love and support! I love you to the moon and back!

ACKNOWLEDGEMENTS

This book would not have been possible without the help of these awesome people:

To my wife, Sarah: You are amazing! Thank you for your support and encouragement throughout this journey! From the day the book became an idea, to writing the first chapter, to deciding to publish it…you have been my biggest fan and I'm forever thankful for you!

To my Kickstarter backers: You guys are awesome! I'm completely blown away by your generosity and support of this project! Seriously, THANK YOU! Special thanks to Cheryl and Wayne Lay, Brenda Butts, Chuck E. Tate, and Jennifer Laskey.

To my publishing team: I'm blessed to have worked with these people! They were awesome to work with and I owe them more than I can say for helping me get this book out into the world. Thanks to Melinda Martin for the outstanding interior design; Casey Hurst for the awesome cover design; Marcy Kompare for taking on this project and helping me with editing; Shayla Raquel for helping me make sure my sources were edited and good to go; and to Jeffrey Dean and Chuck E. Tate for writing a foreword.

Contents

TO REALLY SEE

Those three days must have seemed like an eternity. Nothing to eat, nothing to drink, and if this were not misery enough… blindness too. It was only a short time ago when Saul had stood in agreement and watched as Stephen, a Christian, was murdered.

The present trip he was on had started off so promising for Saul; a routine trip into Damascus with letters from the high priest to arrest, beat, imprison, or possibly kill any person belonging to the "Way." This was to be just another day like the many days previous of ridding the world of Christ-followers.

The bright light changed everything.

I wonder what was more shocking to Saul—not being able to see, or the realization that the Jesus whom he had been persecuting was the one who took his sight from him?

Either way, he was beginning to see that he had it all wrong before. Saul knew that things would never be the same.

Had Saul said "no" to Jesus, would he have remained blind the rest of his life? Would he have continued to try and kill Christians? Would someone else have written the thirteen books of the New

Testament that Paul wrote? Fortunately for him, and for us, he said "yes" to Jesus. Saul became Paul and the rest is history.

This is just one of many stories of redemption in the Bible.

Brokenness to blessing.

Hurt to healing.

Hopelessness to hope.

Sin to salvation.

It's pretty remarkable to think that the Jesus who met Saul on the road to Damascus that day is the same Jesus waiting to meet with you. And, just as was the case with Saul the same is true for you. Your past doesn't define your future when Jesus Christ is in the mix. Jesus took care of your past at the cross.

He has a new story already written for you.

A story worth finding if you choose.

A story worth following if you dare.

A story worth living if you are willing to step into the bright light and possibly begin to see, really see, for the first time in your life.

—Jeffrey Dean
Author of *The Graduate Handbook* (WordView 2013)
JeffreyDean.com

CLEAN SLATE

Several years ago I hopped in my Mini Cooper and drove from Peoria, Illinois to Anderson, South Carolina to attend a pastor/leadership conference at NewSpring Church. My biggest takeaway was the following truth bomb—a drop the mic revelation that we immediately implemented at the church I lead.

Every NUMBER has a name. Every NAME has a story. Every STORY matters to God.

Yassss!

You're more than a number. And regardless of what you might have heard growing up—you're not an accident. God *knew you* and He knew what you would be named before your parents even conceived you.

Jeremiah 1:5 (NLV) confirms this. *"Before I started to put you together in your mother, I knew you. Before you were born, I set you apart as holy. I chose you to speak to the nations for Me."*

As my friend (and author of Reckless Grace) Bill Vanderbush says, "This means that God knew you before you even knew you could be known." Wrap your mind around that for a second. God knows more about you than you even know about yourself.

In Ephesians 2:10, the Apostle Paul (who just so happened to have an encounter with Jesus that transformed his life and rewrote his story) declares that *you* are God's masterpiece. The Passion Translation lays out his words like this: "*...Even before we were born, God planned in advance our destiny and the good works we would do to fulfill it!*"

This means *you* matter.
This means your *story* matters.

Perhaps you feel like God has been silent. Let me remind you that His silence doesn't mean that He is absent. He's involved in your story because you are in His story. In fact, I believe that He is already working behind the scenes to set up divine appointments to redeem your story. And I believe that one of those divine appointments is you picking up this book by my friend Aaron Hall.

As you read the following pages of this book, Aaron is going help you remove the blinders from your eyes so you can see clearly that your identity is in Christ and Christ alone. He's going to show you that regardless of your failures, shortcomings, and setbacks, it's never too late for God to rewrite your story.

Consider this moment a clean slate. Continue reading and let God write something new on the pages of your heart.

—Chuck E. Tate
Author of *41 Will Come* (Tyndale Momentum 2016)
ChuckETate.com

YOU HAVE A STORY

E veryone has a story.

From Genesis to Revelation you see a story of redemption unfolding. Isaiah 47:4 (ESV) says that God is "our Redeemer—the LORD of hosts is his name—is the Holy One of Israel." Since the fall happened in Genesis chapter 3 God has been writing redemption in the lives of countless people. In this book, we will zoom in on a few people in the story of Scripture where God redeemed their story despite their mistakes, guilt, and shame. We will also look at how, even today, God wants to redeem your story too. So, if you're a drug addict reading this: God wants to redeem your story. If you're a struggling alcoholic who's made countless mistakes: God wants to redeem your story. If you had an affair and walked out on your family: God wants to redeem your story. If you've cheated and lied your whole life and it's destroyed your relationships with friends and family: God wants to redeem your story.

Maybe your story is written with unforgiveness and bitterness or anger that has given birth to hatred and resentment. Perhaps your story is written with mistakes that have morphed your guilt into an unbearable shame that's become so heavy you find it hard to even breathe. Let me be upfront with you: this book is about challenging you to let God rewrite your story—to replace anger with joy and shame with freedom. It's a call to give the pen back to the author of creation and allow him to pen a new story from the torn pages of what has become a life of mistakes and shame—a life that *seems* broken beyond repair. I know all about making mistakes, feeling guilty, and living with shame. I also know how the things we have done (or the things that have been done to us) can easily define us—and our story.

One of the coolest things about God is that he doesn't *recreate*. He creates. He doesn't recycle what was bad in order to make something good. When you got saved 2 Corinthians 5:17 (CSB) says this about you: "Therefore, if anyone is in Christ, he is a new creation; the old has passed away, and see, the new has come!" Notice what it *doesn't* say. It doesn't say: "Therefore, if anyone is in Christ, he is a *recreation*; the old has been *recycled*, and the *recreation* has come." No, when you "confess with your mouth that Jesus is Lord and believe in your heart that God raised him from the dead, you will be saved."[1] When you accepted Christ as your Lord and Savior you become a *new* creation. The old life—the old story—has been erased. You are now in a position for God to redeem your story. To rewrite it with a new ending. To write hope instead of fear. To write joy instead of anger. And to write grace instead of condemnation. You are in the place where you can make the choice to give the pen back. You're not a recreation. You're a new creation. Give up the pen and let God create!

The Apostle Paul writes in Titus 2:14 (ESV) about Jesus, that he "gave himself for us to redeem us from all lawlessness and to purify

---

1 Romans 10:9 (ESV).

for himself a people for his own possession who are zealous for good works." Merriam-Webster defines the word *redeem* as "to buy back."[2] Throughout the pages of Scripture, you see God's divine plan unfold to redeem his creation.

From Abraham to King David to the Apostle Paul, and all the other great men and women of the faith, each of their stories is written within the grander story of God *buying back* a broken world. The Bible says in Acts 3:21 (ESV), "...Whom [*speaking of Jesus*] heaven must receive until the time for restoring all the things about which God spoke by the mouth of his holy prophets long ago." By God's grace we get to experience restoration. His divine story of redemption reached its climax when Jesus was mocked, beaten, humiliated, and crucified. But the story is still being told. It isn't over yet, because God doesn't wish that any would "perish but all to come to repentance."[3]

Paul writes in 2 Corinthians 5:21 (ESV), "For our sake he made him to be sin who knew no sin, so that in him we might become the righteousness of God." Jesus was perfect. He willingly chose to take our sin upon himself. To take our place upon the cross. And to endure God's wrath on our behalf. Jesus was betrayed by one of his own disciples, arrested, and then put on trial. The people were ready to kill the very one that came to "seek and to save."[4] They demanded that he be killed and that Barabbas, who was a leader of an insurrection and a murderer, be released instead.

---

2 *Merriam-Webster*, s.v. "redeem(*v.*)" accessed October 10, 2019, https://www.merriam-webster.com/dictionary/redeem
3 2 Peter 3:9 (CSB).
4 Luke 19:10 (NIV).

Giving in to their requests, Pilate "delivered Jesus over to their will."[5] It was the will of the people to crucify Jesus, but it was the will of God to crucify Jesus for the people—that includes you and me. The story of redemption is a beautiful story of grace. Even while they drove those nails into his hands and feet, and raised him up on that cross to humiliate him, Jesus didn't once condemn them. He loved them even then. He doesn't want you to live in a story of regret or shame. He's inviting you into his story of redemption, because it's grace that makes it possible. Without grace, there would be no hope of redemption in creation. I continually thank God for his grace!

It's my hope that you see yourself as someone whom God loves—someone whom God wants to redeem! Your story matters because you matter to God!

I pray you are encouraged by this book and that you'll find redemption written in your story. If you're reading this, it's not too late. There's still hope. No matter what you've done, what you've been through, or what's been done to you. There is hope on the horizon.

---

5 Luke 23:25 (ESV).

CHAPTER 1

ALL PEOPLE, ALL STORIES

I was sitting on the balcony overlooking the canal. My wife and I had gone down to the Florida Keys to spend a few days with her aunt and uncle who were vacationing there. We had just completed serving with three summer camps spanning two states, and had been away from home for much of the summer. We wanted—rather, needed—a few days rest with no work. Just God and family. While I sat out on the balcony, I asked my wife's uncle, "Do most of these people live here year-round?" I was referring to the houses along the canal. He proceeded to tell me who lived here year-round and who didn't. The house directly across the canal was now owned by a seasonal dweller. But the previous owner was a resident of Big Pine Key, Florida. And his name was Dave.

Dave was a retired computer guy who had worked for the government. He was a nice guy—and was completely lost. He also liked to drink a lot. He never got drunk but always had a drink in his hand. He also had a filthy mouth. The f-bomb wasn't foreign to his vocabulary. To be honest, his life story resembles so many of the stories being told all over the world. Dave's a good guy. He hasn't killed anyone or robbed a bank. He just likes to drink a lot and cuss like a sailor. Yeah, he's heaven's definition of a good guy, right? To many, you better believe he is. To God, no he is not. There is no one good apart from God. Any good in a Christian is because of God. Jesus says in Luke 18:19 (ESV), "Why do you call me good? No one is good except God alone." Dave was a "good" guy in the world's eye. To God, he was a man in much need of Jesus. Like I was. Like so many other people still are today.

My wife's uncle proceeded to tell me that one day, while Dave was helping his neighbor work on a boat motor, he decided to hop on his bike and ride around the block to give them a hand. While across the canal my wife's uncle noticed Dave's language had cleaned up and he told him he seemed like a totally different person.

"I found the Lord," Dave said without hesitating. "See those rocks?" There were some rocks along the canal instead of a seawall. He nodded toward them. "I was outside working one day and fell and broke my leg. I laid out there for over two hours before anyone found me. I found the Lord that day."

Dave is just one person on the planet who answered the call to have his story rewritten. That's what this book is all about. The call to have your story rewritten isn't a call that's selective or conditional. If you allow the author and finisher to have control, you too can have your life tell a new story. A better story.

Not only does everyone have a story but every story has the potential to be rewritten. Your story. A drug addict. A thief. A lair. A sexually immoral person. The world has billions of stories from every nation and every culture—stories that matter to God. I find it hard to believe that the God who made every person in his own image desires anything less than for all people to come to Jesus. Of course, I know every story will not be rewritten. I've read Revelation. But every person has the *opportunity* to hand over the pen.

In this first chapter I want to share with you that all people, all stories have the potential to change the world. I want to share with you the stories of two people who come from two different backgrounds. Stories that have gone from darkness to light. From being spiritually dead to being Spirit-filled. Stories that demonstrate that God is not only loving, but diverse and creative when he redeems. Every testimonial story isn't the same. I like to think God does that on purpose. Each of the two stories I will be sharing shows that God is more than able to rewrite what's been poorly written.

This chapter will also explore the story of Jonah, a man who seriously thought he could run away from God. All because he was judgmental and prejudiced. The story of Jonah reveals the grace of God. It reveals that all people, all stories can be redeemed by the very one who penned the opening sentence of every story and knows when the final chapter will be written.

Ava's Story

> "And the LORD appointed a great fish to swallow
> up Jonah. And Jonah was in the belly of the fish
> three days and three nights." —Jonah 1:17 (ESV)

God used a great fish to change the direction of Jonah's story. Perhaps it was because God knew it was going to take drastic measures to turn him around. Living in the belly of a big fish for three days and three nights would surely get my attention! I believe God can use whatever means he deems necessary to reach people…to get our attention. For Jonah, it was a fish. For the Apostle Paul, it was a blinding light on the road to Damascus. For one of my students it was an awareness of the darkness around her. For her privacy, her name and some of the details of her story have been changed. The changes don't at all subtract from the overall redeeming message Ava's story brings. It's my prayer her story encourages you to answer the call to have your story rewritten if you haven't already.

For several summers, I took my youth group to summer camp at Lake Placid Camp and Conference Center in Lake Placid, Florida. It's about a forty-minute drive from where we are in Okeechobee. The night before students arrived, several of us would drive over to set everything up and to pray over each bunk bed. While the band finished setting up the stage, I went into the boy's dorm to pray. While in there the Holy Spirit told me to pray for breakthrough and then brought to mind the story of Jericho in Joshua 6.

In my ESV Bible, chapter 6 is given the title: *The Fall of Jericho*. If you don't know the story, I'll give you Aaron's paraphrased version. The people of Israel are told by God through Joshua to circle Jericho seven times—once per day—and on the seventh day they were told to march around Jericho seven times. "Seven priests shall bear seven trumpets of rams' horns before the ark. On the seventh day you shall march around the city seven times, and the priests shall blow the trumpets. And when they make a long blast with the ram's horn, when you hear the sound of the trumpet, then all the people shall shout with a great shout, and the wall of the city will fall down flat, and the people shall go up, everyone straight before him."[6] While praying in the dorm, the Lord revealed to me that many of the students who would occupy both the boys' and girls' dorms had walls up like the city of Jericho. Walls that needed to come down. Walls that Jesus wanted to break through.

Some who will read this book will have walls up that they are protecting—walls that Jesus wants to knock down to bring healing, hope, redemption. Jonah had a wall of prejudice up that needed to come down. I've had a wall of fear up that needed to come down. I have a friend who had a wall of people pleasing up that needed to come down. Just because a wall is torn down doesn't mean it can't be rebuilt. Many times, we have breakthroughs, but over time we revert back to the rubble and begin to rebuild the wall. A lasting breakthrough requires us to press forward with Jesus and to continue to press forward once we are beyond the wall. We can't look back at the destruction like Lot's wife did when she turned and looked back at Sodom and Gomorrah and was turned into salt. If we go back to the walls and begin to rebuild them the same thing can happen to our hearts. We must look ahead. We must look toward Jesus. We must run with Jesus.

When we prayed for these walls to come down, the leaders and I were praying against whatever came through the gates of hell against our students and us. While writing this chapter I shared with one of our camp sponsors what I was writing, and she told me this: "Your team's intercession before sets up shields around the camp." We prayed in unity, lifting up our shields of faith to protect what the Lord was doing and was going to do. The enemy of our souls wanted nothing more than to derail what God purposed to take

---

6 Joshua 6:4–5 (ESV).

place at camp. Ava's story proves that the shields held up and that not even the forces of hell can keep Jesus from bringing deliverance when someone cries out for him to be their Lord and Savior.

Ava comes from a rough family. Her home life isn't glamorous. She comes from a home where darkness runs uninterrupted. Every little girl needs to hear from her dad that she is loved. That she is valued. That she is beautiful. Ava didn't get that. Her home life was a severe downgrade from what a majority of my students live in. I know there are students in my youth group that come from broken homes. Some worse than others.

We had been at Lake Placid for several nights. Up until this point we had had some students get saved and others find freedom. Walls were coming down! But there was still breakthrough that needed to happen.

It was late. I was in my bunk when my wife called me to come out to the sanctuary. It was around one in the morning. I went out there to find her and two of our youth leaders sitting around a table eating, talking, laughing. I joined them and we began to share some of the things we had seen God do so far with some of the students. Some of the things were hilarious. Some were serious. After about twenty minutes I decided to head back to bed because 7AM was only a few hours away.

The day before, Ava's sister had gotten really sick. Their family hadn't been able to afford the cost of summer camp, so the girls were sponsored. The woman who sponsored them loved these girls. She prayed for them like a loving mother. She embraced them. Encouraged them. She even drove forty minutes to camp to pick up Ava's sister because she was sick and drove her back home to Fort Pierce, which was about an hour and a half drive from camp. Ava wanted to go home too, but my wife told her no. That she really felt like the Lord wanted her to stay. Ava listened and decided she should stay (we don't let students just leave camp simply because they want to).

This is where Ava's story gets interesting. My wife had gone back to her dorm as well. Unbeknownst to me at the time, when my wife was walking back to her bed down the dark hallway, Ava jumped out of nowhere, taking hold of my wife and saying with much fear and trembling, "Sarah! You gotta believe me!"

Needless to say, my wife was startled (I would have been too)! But if the story God was penning startled Sarah and shook Ava to a breaking point, it was in order to push Ava's story in the direction of grace and redemption. Let me explain.

Ava held onto my wife while she explained: She had been laying in her own bed, but she felt like something was pressing down on her. She found it hard to breathe. She was terrified. Who wouldn't be? She then told my wife she had a vision and saw darkness all around her—demons coming at her. She mentioned she even felt like someone was hitting her in the stomach. She tried to scream but she couldn't talk. She was silenced by fear. But then something like a window of light appeared and the darkness fled immediately!

The demonic oppression she experienced was real. The Bible says in Ephesians 6:12 (ESV), "For we do not wrestle against flesh and blood, but against the rulers, against the authorities, against the cosmic powers over this present darkness, against the spiritual forces of evil in the heavenly places." Ava wasn't wrestling with flesh and blood while lying in her bed! She was wrestling with the present darkness—the demonic forces that are charged with plotting against her story in every way possible.

Ava was confused, scared, and didn't really understand what that light represented. My wife explained to her that at the mention of Jesus' name demons must flee. She point-blank asked her if she even knew Jesus. Ava admitted she didn't have a personal relationship with Jesus as her Lord and Savior. My wife then got to pray with her and led her to Jesus right there in that dark dorm at two o'clock in the morning.

God appointed a great fish for Jonah. That fish pushed Jonah toward the people of Nineveh, which led to a city-wide revival! I believe God allowed Ava to be aware of the darkness around her to push her toward Jesus. A dark story was rewritten with hope that night. Sometimes God allows certain things to get our attention. To open our eyes so we can see we all are born with a Jesus-shaped hole that only he can fill. I firmly believe that. This is only the start of a new story for Ava. Pray for her as she learns what it means to walk with Jesus.

❖

Like I mentioned earlier in this chapter, the story of Jonah reveals the grace of God.

Maybe you're like Jonah and you're running. Jonah thought it was humanly possible to run "away from the presence of the LORD."[7]

---

7 Jonah 1:3b (ESV).

The beauty of grace is it will meet you right where you are no matter how long you've been running or how far you've gone to turn your story into a mess. Grace isn't bound by time. It can reach you no matter where you are in the world. It can reach a young child and someone in their late eighties on their deathbed.

Grace knows no skin color, is not bound by cultural differences, and is not prejudiced. Grace is free and freely offered to all who come to Jesus Christ.

That's right. It's offered to all people. The cross wasn't for some and not others. For God so loved the world... that covers you, me, and everyone else! Grace is offered to that murderer who got life in prison. It's offered to that closet alcoholic who can't seem to stop. It was offered to all those people in Nineveh. Despite how I feel about someone or how Jonah felt about the Ninevites, God loves all people and the Bible is clear that God "is not slow to fulfill his promise as some count slowness, but is patient toward you, not wishing that any should perish, but that all should reach repentance."[8]

Grace is even offered to people like Adolf Hitler. *Whoa*! Crazy to think about, right? Trust me, I know it is, especially because he's responsible for killing millions of Jews and for initiating World War II. But let me tell you, if he would have truly repented and turned to Jesus at any point in his life do you think God would have redeemed his story? I believe so. Maybe you're thinking, no! There's no way God would have! Hitler was too wicked of a man! I couldn't agree more, *but* grace isn't limited to only people who are good in our own definition of what is good and what is evil. Grace can flood

---

8 2 Peter 3:9 (ESV).

the darkest of hearts and bring life change through Jesus. Grace isn't prejudiced to any certain type of sinner. Did God not spare the Ninevites when Jonah shared the message God gave him? It was a picture of grace. Grace wins…if you choose it—*Jesus*—of course.

No matter what commandment you've broken in your story grace is able to redeem it.

Any story can be redeemed. Any story includes your story!

Even when Jonah ran away, God pursued him. God loves all people—this included every single person in Nineveh. Jesus didn't die for just a certain group of people. His sacrifice was for all who would believe and trust in him. God didn't love Jonah less because he acted out in his flesh and allowed his judgmental heart and prejudice toward the people of Nineveh to write a few pages of his story. There's nothing you could do to make God love you less. God loves you and me and even people like Jeffrey Dahmer. Sin separates us from God and it breaks fellowship with God. Because God loves you he offers grace, which can wash the blackest of sin white as snow. It's said that Jeffrey Dahmer gave his life to Christ before he was killed in prison. I don't know if that's true, but if it is then grace washed his sin away and he's with Jesus today. Grace will reach any person that turns to Jesus.

I believe God gives second chances. Jonah 3:1–2 (CSB) tells us that "the word of the LORD came to Jonah a second time: 'Get up! Go to the great city of Ninevah and preach the message that I tell you.'" The cool thing is even if you have messed up more than twice, grace isn't limited to just two times. God will never turn away a heart that truly repents.

Grace isn't a ticket to sin more. So, don't hear me wrong. I don't believe in "greasy grace," or abusing God's grace to continue in sin.

We must live dead to sin. We shouldn't live to entertain any kind of sin thinking grace will cover us. Paul writes in Romans 6:11–14 (ESV), "So you also must consider yourselves dead to sin and alive to God in Christ Jesus. Let not sin therefore reign in your mortal body, to make you obey its passions. Do not present your members to sin as instruments for unrighteousness, but present yourselves to God as those who have been brought from death to life, and your members to God as instruments for righteousness. For sin will have no dominion over you, since you are not under law but under grace." "*Under grace*" doesn't mean you can or should abuse grace. Grace is a gift that some people misuse. Don't misuse it as a free pass to live like hell and still expect to reflect Christ to the world.

God had threatened to destroy Nineveh if the people did not turn from their wicked ways. After Jonah was obedient and went to the great city to preach the word the Lord had given him, Scripture tells us that "When God saw their actions—that they had turned from their evil ways—He relented from the disaster He had threatened to bring upon them."[9]

Anyone who doesn't repent and believe in Jesus Christ as their Lord and Savior will face the judgment and wrath of God for their wickedness. No matter what wickedness you have committed, God longs for you to repent. If grace reached the people of Nineveh it can reach you right where you are now. Grace can be written into any story.

---

9 Jonah 3:10 (BSB).

Grace reached Peter when he denied the Lord Jesus three times publicly. Grace reached Paul even after he approved of Stephen's murder. Grace reached me even after I ran from God for so many years—even after I chased religion rather than a personal relationship with Jesus.

So how do you receive grace? By faith (see Ephesians 2:8)! Grace is God's free and unmerited favor. It's God giving us what we don't deserve. It's different than mercy. Mercy is deliverance from judgment. God can write grace (and mercy) into your story. He's that good! Take a moment to spend some time with the Lord. Put this book down, grab your Bible and get alone with God. Repent of any known sin, worship him, thank him and watch how he lavishes his presence over you. He's a gracious God.

My Story

As I write this, I just got home from a men's retreat that my home church put on. While there, I heard the Holy Spirit tell me I should include my story in this chapter. Many times, when we think of someone who ran from God, we automatically think of someone who perhaps once knew God and then ran and lived wild. I know many people who were prodigals in that sense and have since found the embracing arms of our heavenly Father. My story is different... maybe it's like yours or someone you know. Regardless, if the Lord nudged me to tell it here then I know it is for a purpose. And I trust him.

I grew up in a home that really didn't practice any religion; but if you asked, we were that typical American Christian family.

We owned a Bible. We went to church on Easter and sometimes on Christmas Eve. But our words didn't align with our actions. Knowing what it means today to have a real relationship with Jesus, I can tell you that we were far from being authentic Christians. But like us, so many people put Christianity on their Facebook profiles as if it's just the thing you do. Jesus isn't their Lord and Savior. They only want him when they hit a hard spot in life or someone they know dies. Then they want prayer or they attempt to pray themselves. That was me. Christianity is so much more than that. It's not about having a religion. It's about having an authentic relationship with Jesus as Lord *and* Savior.

On my mom's side of the family there were several Old Regular Baptist preachers. Growing up I heard about God, the cross, heaven and hell. I was convinced at an early age that if you didn't believe in Santa Claus then you didn't believe in Jesus. Sounds innocent, but my distorted belief was never corrected. Now I didn't grow up believing in Santa for long! I stopped when I was around nine, but Jesus never became someone I couldn't live without because the Jesus I knew was a version I crafted over the years—a version that said I was right with God when in reality I was far from God.

I lived dead until I was twenty years old.

Wait, *what?* I know it sounds weird to say someone "lived dead" but isn't that all of us before we come to Jesus? Aren't we all spiritually dead? Ephesians 2:1 (GNT) says, "In the past you were spiritually dead because of your disobedience and sins." My version of who I believed Jesus to be couldn't save me from my "disobedience and sins". On the outside I looked like a good person—good in the world's sense. But God's Word makes it clear that there is no one good.[10] The only good in me today is Jesus. Apart from Christ there is nothing good in me.

If all you pursue is religion then you will live spiritually dead, *unless* you encounter the radical love of Jesus and he becomes Savior and Lord over every area of your life. Religion offers empty promises but Jesus offers hope, peace, forgiveness, freedom, restoration, life. I chased after religion until I was twenty years old because I didn't know any better. I don't think I ever really heard a clear presentation of the gospel growing up, because I sincerely believe if I had I likely wouldn't have lived so long without Jesus!

I was running from God for twenty years and I didn't even know it. Jonah knew he was trying to flee the presence of God. Psalm 139 (ESV) says that God is omnipresent, meaning there is no place where he doesn't exist:

> Where shall I go from your Spirit?
> Or where shall I flee from your presence?
> If I ascend to heaven, you are there!
> If I make my bed in Sheol, you are there!
> If I take the wings of the morning
> and dwell in the uttermost parts of the sea,
> even there your hand shall lead me,
> and your right hand shall hold me (verses 7–10).

We can't hide or run from God. We may think we can, but it's kind of hard to run or hide from someone who is everywhere past, present, and future!

You see, my version of Jesus blinded me to the truth of who

---

10 See Psalm 53:5.

I was running from and the direction I was truly running. Maybe that's you. Maybe that's someone you know.

In high school, I dated a girl but that relationship didn't bring any glory or honor to God. I had friends who drank and it would be a lie to tell you that I never drank with them. I was the billboard for hypocrisy. If anyone asked me, I was good with God and headed toward heaven. But yet I never read my Bible, went to church (apart from the occasional visit), or lived a life that pointed anyone to Jesus. I would sneak around with my girlfriend, entertain idols such as music, and drink with friends occasionally, all the while praying every night before I went to bed without repenting of my sin. My prayers were self-centered. They were always about me, for my benefit, and to help me sleep at night knowing how I lived each day. I think deep down I knew something was missing, but it was buried so deep that my version of Jesus allowed me to put on a facade, pretending that I was good when I really wasn't at all. To some who know me, some of what I just said about who I really was in school might come as a shock. Maybe you can relate. Perhaps your story is like mine. You've pursued religion for so long but now you're realizing that you're actually spiritually dead and in much need of a Savior. His name is Jesus, and "there is salvation in no one else, for there is no other name under heaven given among men by which we must be saved."[11]

The church where I discovered the real Jesus no longer exists. It has since been torn down and now State Road 70 runs right through where I once knelt down at the altar to make Jesus Lord and Savior of my story. It was a tiny little church on the outskirts

---

11 Acts 4:12 (ESV).

of town called House of Refuge. Less than thirty people were there the night I went. I didn't come when my friend first invited me. The week before I had made up an excuse not to go. I wanted to watch a new show that was airing on TV and I lied about my back hurting. But the next week I didn't have any legitimate reason as to why I couldn't go. So, I went. And the Aaron that walked in the front door that night never came back. Here's what happened that night on October 29, 2009: *I went from being spiritually dead to being Spirit-filled.* What I mean by Spirit-filled isn't that I broke out in tongues or started acting weirdly. And for the record, the Holy Spirit isn't weird. I would recommend to anyone with questions about the Holy Spirit to read Robert Morris' book *The God I Never Knew* if you really want to understand how being friends with the Holy Spirit can radically change your life. The Bible says in 1 Corinthians 6:19 (CSB), "Don't you know that your body is a temple of the Holy Spirit who is in you, whom you have from God? You are not your own." When Jesus made me a new creation that night, he not only resurrected my dead spirit but his Spirit made his home in me. I became "Spirit-filled." I could write a whole book on what it means to live the "Spirit-filled life." This isn't that book. Maybe one day I will, if the Lord leads me to do so.

Anyhow, I was sitting in my chair listening to the sermon Pastor Brian was preaching. I can't remember exactly what he was saying other than he was talking about worship. The Lord began to tug on my spirit. I realized in that moment my life didn't at all worship God or honor him in any way. Jesus says about the Holy Spirit in John 16:8–11 (CSB), "When he comes, he will convict the world about sin, righteousness, and judgment: About sin, because they do not believe in me; about righteousness, because I am going to the

Father and you will no longer see me; and about judgment, because the ruler of this world has been judged." The Lord convicted me of my sin—that I was pursuing my own version of who I believed Jesus to be. My heart was racing. It felt like it was going to jump out of my chest. I was wrestling with going to the altar because I already knew Jesus… I was already a Christian, remember? But why then did I have this emptiness inside? Why then did I feel like the Holy Spirit was calling me and telling me, "Aaron, you need me. Come." Why then did I sense in my spirit that I was not in right standing with God at all?

I found myself standing up, drawn to the love of a heavenly Father I had never really known, and walking up front. The moment my knees hit the floor I began to cry out to Jesus to be Lord and Savior of my life. I couldn't hold back the tears. I wasn't crying because I was upset, I was crying because for the first time in my life I was convinced that my sin separated me from God and that if I died I would go to hell. I was convinced that I needed Jesus. I was convinced that only Jesus (the real biblical Jesus) could make me be in right standing with God.

That night I went from being an enemy of God to a friend of God!

This was the moment my story changed directions. I handed over the pen and God began to tell a new story. My story was redeemed—bought back because of Jesus and the blood he spilled at Calvary for me. I find myself back at the altar often, not because I need to get saved again but because sometimes I mess up and try to take the pen back and write my story. I repent often, because it would be a lie to say that after coming to Christ I don't sin. We all do. Everyday Jesus writes a new sentence, a new chapter. And I'm thankful for that!

Before I left church that night my friend said to me, "Now that you're saved Satan is going to try and attack you." I still had much pride and brushed his words off as if saying, "That isn't going to happen to me." Satan tried to hijack my story when my parents separated just two days later, when I lost my financial aid for college a few months later, and when my car died within a year after my story was redeemed. God can redeem your story and Satan will try and hijack it. Life may not have gotten easier after coming to Jesus, but I knew God was writing a better story and the best thing I can do is trust him as the author. Thank God that "the one who is in you is greater than the one who is in the world."[12]

My story had a much different ending than Jonah's story, though my story is still being written. Like yours. Jonah ended up being angry at the fact that God relented from destroying the people of Nineveh. I can't say it enough: the story of Jonah reveals the grace of God. I'm thankful God's grace reached me even when I was pursuing the wrong Jesus and running in the wrong direction. As I sit here and write this I can't help but think that, perhaps, there is someone out there who will read this book and see that their story isn't over. That God is not finished penning a new chapter in their life. That their story is like Ava's or mine or that they will see the potential they have in Christ. And because of that they will not allow depression, anger, fear, regret, shame, etcetera to write the final chapter of their story. Maybe they too will answer the call like Ava

---

12 1 John 4:4b (CSB).

and I and so many others have done to have their story redeemed—bought back with a new plot, a new purpose, a new story.

Maybe it's time for you to answer the call, because everyone has a story and every story matters to God! Trust me, no matter how bad your story has become God can redeem it.

CHAPTER 2

YOUR PAIN

Jesse was the same age as me when he stepped into eternity. He was also my cousin. The pain I felt losing my cousin paled in comparison to what my Aunt Brenda was feeling. The loss of a child is a pain that cuts deep and leaves a scar that lasts a lifetime. I want to open up this chapter with her story. I'll let her tell you in her own words about how even when losing her son, God was more than able to "work together for good"[13] what happened on July 10th, 2013. And in doing so, she realized even in her pain God can redeem the story.

Brenda's Story

I felt like I had died and they forgot to bury me. There is nothing more devastating than losing a child. All your hopes and dreams for that child are gone. There is an ache in your gut from the pain. I never got mad at God but I questioned and yelled at Him a lot.

I had been told on Monday night, July 8, 2013, that Jesse had been without enough oxygen too long and it would be a miracle if he woke up. So, I began to pray that night through Tuesday for

13 Romans 8:28 (ESV).

God to show those doctors a miracle. My faith was unwavering that Tuesday afternoon. There were several doctors in the room with us and Jesse. One of the doctors said, "Is he following me?" I looked over and Jesse was awake. He was following all of us with his eyes! His vitals had all stabilized even though he was on the ventilator, he responded to what I said appropriately and even gave the doctors thumbs up. We stayed for several more hours and then went home because we had been there from Monday night until Tuesday evening. I had such a peace in my heart when I went home that evening.

The next morning around 6:00 a.m. or so, the hospital called and said they were coding Jesse. His heart had stopped. They had been coding him for a while. I asked them to continue and we left for the hospital. I received the call on the way there: "We have coded Jesse for over 45 minutes and there is no response!"

I was in shock for several days—planning his funeral and taking care of things. I remember a dream I had a week or so before where Jesse had opened the front door of the house and outside was total darkness and it was storming. The darkness tried to suck him out of the door, but he bulked up and hung on and it did not take him out. At the time, I thought it meant he would beat his illness. Now I know it was showing me Satan was fighting for his soul and lost.

The weeks and months following Jesse's death were horrible. I have never been in such a dark place. I really thought I would die and I wanted to die! All joy was gone. I could not even look at my Bible. On one hand I was relieved for him, his battle was over, but I wondered how many years I would live without him in this pain. I left his room untouched for over a year with all the pictures from the funeral on the walls. I cried every time I thought of him. Slowly I started reading Scripture again and watching sermons about heaven. The more I read and watched sermons, the more peace I had. Now more than ever, even several years later, I still get depressed and cry, though not as often. I can talk about him without crying. I focus on heaven now and the promises of God. I still question why sometimes but I know I will see him again.[14]

❖

You may think your pain can't be redeemed… that because of your pain God can't write a new story. A new story full of healing, hope, and purpose. If every story matters to God then it makes sense to believe that even in your pain, God is more than able to pen a new beginning. It makes sense to believe that even in the midst of the unimaginable—like the loss of a child, a parent or being served divorce papers—God is able to rewrite what you may have written as the storyline of your life.

Regardless of how you encountered your pain, God can redeem it for his glory. Your story can be redeemed even if the pain you are suffering was caused by a choice or decision you made or if it was beyond your ability to control. In this chapter, we will look at the story of Job. Job lost everything. His kids. His health. His possessions. But even in his pain, he refused to curse God. He trusted God in the midst of unimaginable pain—pain that many who read this book might be experiencing as well. The loss of a child, a parent or a friend. Maybe your health is declining. Maybe you're struggling, lost your job and have lost everything. Job's story shows us God can redeem your pain and rewrite hope in a story full of hurt. This chapter

---

14 The section titled "Brenda's Story" was written by Brenda Butts.

builds off of the fact that God wants to rewrite your pain (whether physical, emotional or even mental) with unshakeable faith so that you can live a story full of grace and purpose.

Maybe you're reading this and you're like my Aunt Brenda. You've lost a child. The pain is deep, numbing, and heartbreaking. And though I can't relate to it specifically, people like my Aunt Brenda can; and her story is proof that even in that moment of unimaginable darkness God can shine light, redeem, and give your story hope again.

I don't think it's a coincidence that God included in his grand story of redemption—his Word—a story of a man who lost all of his children. God's Word can speak to you right where you are in your story, because "the word of God is living and active, sharper than any two-edged sword, piercing to the division of soul and spirit, of joints and of marrow, and discerning the thoughts and intentions of the heart."[15] The one who gives the words of the Bible such power is the very one who can change everything in your story.

Let's take a look a Job's story.

❖

When bad things happen to bad people, we generally don't bat an eye. When bad things happen to good people, however, many begin to question God in the aftermath. The Bible says in Job 1:1–3 (ESV), "There was a man in the land of Uz whose name was Job, and that man was blameless and upright, one who feared God and turned away from evil. There were born to him seven sons and three daughters. He possessed 7,000 sheep, 3,000 camels, 500 yoke of

---

15 Hebrews 4:12 (ESV).

oxen, and 500 female donkeys, and very many servants, so that this man was the greatest of all the people of the east." Job was blameless and upright. That doesn't mean he was perfect. He was a man who feared God and walked intimately with God. He was extremely blessed. I mean, God's Word labeled him as "the greatest of all the people of the east." He was faithful to God and was quite wealthy. Job had everything. Maybe you had everything. Maybe you didn't. Regardless, like Job, many of you—I would bet all of you—reading this book have experienced some kind of pain in your life. We can look to Job and learn from how he responded to the pain he endured.

Job would "rise early in the morning and offer burnt offerings according to the number of them all [*his children*]" and this was something that "Job did regularly."[16] He was a godly man through and through and Satan made it his mission to attack Job's character. Satan had appeared before the Lord in chapter 1 of Job and the Lord said to him, "Have you considered my servant Job? No one else on earth is like him, a man of perfect integrity, who fears God and turns away from evil" (CSB). A little later in the conversation the Lord says to Satan in regards to Job, "Behold, all that he has is in your hand. Only against him do not stretch out your hand"(Job 1:12 ESV).

I want to clarify something that some who read this book might be thinking. *God is sovereign and in control, yet everything that happens isn't always God's doing. Sometimes there are things he permits to happen, but he is not the author of what happens.* God didn't kill my cousin. He permitted his death to happen, because I believe it was his time. The Bible says in Ecclesiastes 3:2 (NIV) that it is appointed

---

16 Job 1:5 (NKJV), with author clarification.

to man "a time to be born, and a time to die." The death of my cousin resulted in my uncle going to church, coming to Christ, and being baptized. I believe God knew that Jesse's death would have a positive impact and push others toward Jesus. God can use your pain to push others toward Jesus.

We don't always see the big picture. But God does. The life of Job shows us that even someone who is blameless and upright and shuns evil can have bad things happen to them. That doesn't mean it's God's fault. We live in a fallen world. We honestly can't expect anything less than bad things to happen in an imperfect world.

After Satan leaves the presence of the Lord in Job 1:12, Job 1:13 begins the section that talks about Job losing his property and children. Let's take a look at it, shall we?

> [13]One day when Job's sons and daughters were eating and drinking wine in their oldest brother's house, [14]a messenger came to Job and reported: "While the oxen were plowing and the donkeys grazing nearby, [15]the Sabeans swooped down and took them away. They struck down the servants with the sword, and I alone have escaped to tell you!"

> [16]He was still speaking when another messenger came and reported: "God's fire fell from heaven. It burned the sheep and the servants and devoured them, and I alone have escaped to tell you!"

> [17]That messenger was still speaking when yet an-

other came and reported: "The Chaldeans formed three bands, made a raid on the camels, and took them away. They struck down the servants with the sword, and I alone have escaped to tell you!"

¹⁸He was still speaking when another messenger came and reported: "Your sons and daughters were eating and drinking wine in their oldest brother's house. ¹⁹Suddenly a powerful wind swept in from the desert and struck the four corners of the house. It collapsed on the young people so that they died, and I alone have escaped to tell you!"

²⁰Then Job stood up, tore his robe, and shaved his head. He fell to the ground and worshiped, ²¹saying:

Naked I came from my mother's womb, and naked I will leave this life. The Lord gives, and the Lord takes away. Blessed be the name of the Lord. ²²Throughout all this Job did not sin or blame God for anything. (Job 1:13-22 CSB)

I love verse 22. Even when Job lost all his property and all ten of his children *he did not blame God*! That's huge! How often, when we are in pain, do we blame God? The truth is many times that's the first reaction to our pain, when our first reaction should be, "How can I let God use this for his glory?"

Maybe it's not emotional. Maybe your pain is physical. Maybe you were in a bad car accident, and you will now have back and neck problems for the rest of your life, because someone decided one night they would get behind the wheel and not think twice about the consequences of driving drunk. Now you blame God for your pain, for not stopping the drunk driver. My Aunt Brenda said in her story: "The weeks and months following Jesse's death were horrible. I have never been in such a dark place. I really thought I would die and I wanted to die! All joy was gone. I could not even look at my Bible." She could have easily blamed God for not helping the doctors save Jesse—to keep Jesse here with us rather than taking him home. She could have chosen to be angry at God, but instead she pushed through it trusting God in her pain. He was there to comfort her through it. And he wants to do the same for you in whatever you are going through that's hurting you. So often when we are in pain we want to run from the very one who can bring us comfort.

The loss of a child is terrible. But you're not alone in your pain. God gave up his one and only son so that we could find salvation, hope, healing, freedom. Why is it you run from him and blame him when bad things happen? I think many times it's because we lose sight of the fact that God is our heavenly Father who loves us so much he sent his son to die a sinner's death for us so that we didn't have to. So when the pain comes, our finite minds blame God, because in our foolish wisdom we think we know what's best. Perhaps God permitted your pain to bring about something far greater, something that would ultimately have an eternal impact. One day we will see and understand why, but while we are on this side of heaven let us not blame the one who gave up everything… the one who longs to rewrite your pain for a purpose greater than yourself.

I decided to add this chapter in this book because of a question I was asked a few years ago when I still worked in retail. I was walking out of the offices after a meeting when a fellow associate approached me. She knew I was a Christian. Her question was more like an accusation against God. Her question was, though not verbatim, "What would you say to someone whose son took his own life?" When her son was alive she went to church. She was serving in the children's ministry. She appeared to be like many other Christians. Happy, serving, loving life. But then everything changed when her son took his life. She was suddenly immersed in the worst pain imaginable for any parent—the loss of her child. The pain of losing her son caused her to abandon church and blame God.

She chose to let her pain write her story. To my knowledge, she hasn't gone back to church to this day. That breaks my heart and I hope and pray you are not in that same place. Instead of running away from God, run toward him. I promise you won't regret it.

My Aunt Brenda let her pain push her toward the one who could rewrite it for good. She's walking more closely with the Lord now than when my cousin was alive. Her story has been redeemed despite the pain that was every bit overwhelming.

Even when Job's children were killed he "did not sin or blame God for anything."[17] The key to letting God rewrite your story is learning to trust him even in the midst of your pain.

Your pain can push you toward God or away from God. It's your choice.

---

17 Job 1:22 (CSB).

❖

For most people pain turns their world upside down. That's what happened to my mom when my grandpa passed away when I was in middle school. Here's her story in her own words:

Fran's Story

My dad's illness and death really changed my life forever. I was raised up in church and I knew when a person dies, if they are saved, they go to be with Jesus. The day my dad passed away, October 18, 2002, my life was completely turned upside down. I was holding my dad's hand when he left this world. My dad had suffered so many months and I was relieved he was out of pain, but, I wanted him here with us.

I had spent the last few months helping Mom take care of Dad. Dad was a hard patient to take care of during his illness. I know many times Mom and I would get frustrated because he would not listen. *Patience* is what God was trying to teach both of us… we had to pray many times for strength, but God always helped us through these situations.

I began looking at the Bible more thoroughly and reading more about heaven so I would know more about where my dad had gone.

I questioned God a lot during this time. I had a dear friend who said to me one day, "at least you had him 38 years, I lost my dad when I was 19." This really hit home. I was not the first daughter to lose her father and I had to be thankful for the 38 years I did have with him. I cried many times as I would be driving to work in the mornings. I knew I had to get closer to God. I had drifted away after I married and I let the material things in life take over. The more I read the Bible, the more I felt at peace.

Thankfully, I worked with many Christians who guided me to verses in the Bible to answer many of my questions. Without my faith in Jesus Christ I do not know how I would have made it through this difficult time. I think of my dad often, especially on his birthday or anniversary of when he went to heaven. I can talk about him now and I have such a peace, because I know that he is in a much better place and that I will see him again one day.[18]

❖

If everyone has their own story then it makes sense to assume that not everyone experiences the same pain. Some will never endure the pain of losing a child. Some will never endure the pain of losing everything, getting fired, or being betrayed by a best friend. Pain can come in many forms and in many different ways. For my mom, it was the declining health of my grandpa.

Job experienced health problems. In verse 6 of Job 2 (NKJV), the Lord tells Satan, "He [Job] is in your hand, but spare his life." Verse 7 goes on to say that "Satan went out from the presence of the Lord, and struck Job with painful boils from the sole of his foot to the crown of his head." That sounds horrible! The physical pain on top of the emotional pain of having lost everything would be astronomical.

Here Job, having already lost his property (and more importantly, all of his children), now has his health struck with something

---

18 The section titled "Fran's Story" was written by Fran Hall.

quite painful. Let's be honest, most people would break under that amount of pain. Most people would raise an angry fist at God. Most people wouldn't think or even dare to believe that God can take even the worst pain and redeem it with purpose.

Let me be clear: God didn't strike Job with these boils. Satan did. I'm not suggesting everything bad that happens is a direct result of Satan. Remember, we live in a fallen world. Yes, Satan is the ruler of this world but sometimes he can just sit back and watch us destroy ourselves. I think that too often we give Satan too much credit. Stop dwelling on how and why you're experiencing this pain and focus on the one who can redeem it: Jesus! He is the only one who can redeem your pain.

Job's wife said to him after he was struck with these terrible boils, "Do you still hold fast your integrity? Curse God and die!" (Job 2:9 NKJV). Job's response to his wife was, "You speak as one of the foolish women speaks. Shall we indeed accept good from God, and shall we not accept adversity?" (Job 2:10 NKJV). Verse ten continues to say that "in all this Job did not sin with his lips."[19] Again, even in his pain Job withheld from blaming God. Job wasn't some super Christian with a heightened ability to endure pain. No, I think it's because he understood the truth that God is good. The world we live in may be far from perfect and full of evil, but that does not void the reality that God is good. Even in your pain it's possible to know and believe that God is good. Satan would have you believe that your pain is because God is not good. Catch the lie,

---

19 Job 2:10b (NKJV).

denounce it, and stay plugged into God's Word and allow the Holy Spirit to "guide you into all the truth."[20]

My grandpa's physical pain was my mom's emotional pain. My Aunt Brenda was angry when Jesse died. My mom was angry when my grandpa died. Job was angry because of all that happened to him. Who wouldn't be angry? Job lost more than many of us have. I can't imagine the pain. But God knows!

❖

More often than not we want God to use his power to heal us here and now to take away our pain on this side of heaven. It's a great thing to pray and ask the Lord for healing. To take away your pain. And I encourage you to pray for healing. But we must also acknowledge the fact that God is ultimately in control and whether or not he heals us of our pain shouldn't deter us from trusting him. Sometimes we won't know why God heals one person but not another. Honestly, that's not for us to know. We can trust that the one who created the universe knows what's best when it comes to healing one person but not another. Our finite minds will never fully grasp the infinite wisdom of God. And that is okay. We all might not be healed of our pain on this side of heaven but one day everyone who puts their faith in Jesus Christ as their personal Lord and Savior will be healed when we get to spend forever with him. Jesse was healed when he went to be with Jesus. My grandpa was healed when he went to be with Jesus. My Aunt Brenda was healed by trusting Jesus through her pain. My mom was healed by trusting Jesus even in the darkness moments of her life. Each wasn't exactly how they wanted but, again, God knows what's best.

20 John 16:13 (CSB).

❖

I love that the book of Job ends with Job's repentance and resto-ration. I also love how the book of Job reveals the humanness of Job—that he wasn't some super Christian who was able to do things we can't. No, he served the same God we serve today.

God redeemed Job's story. One of the cool things about God is when he redeems a story it's not always the same. What I mean by that is everyone has a story, but not every story is the same. We all experience salvation the same way, but sometimes there are differ-ent outcomes that happen as a result of God rewriting our stories because we each have a calling, a purpose that is unique to each of us. My Aunt Brenda's story is different than my mom's and both are different than mine. And, most likely, they will be different from yours. God is creative and I love how each story he rewrites is an original and not an imitation or recreation.

Job 42:12–17 (ESV) says that "the LORD blessed the latter days of Job more than his beginning. And he had 14,000 sheep, 6,000 camels, 1,000 yoke of oxen, and 1,000 female donkeys. He had also seven sons and three daughters. And he called the name of the first daughter Jemimah, and the name of the second Keziah, and the name of the third Keren-happuch. And in all the land there were no women so beautiful as Job's daughters. And their father gave them an inheritance among their brothers. And after this Job lived 140 years, and saw his sons, and his sons' sons, four generations. And Job died, an old man, and full of days."

When God redeemed Job's story his possessions doubled from what is mentioned in Job 1. He was blessed with seven more sons and three more daughters (who apparently were extremely beautiful), and he even got to see four generations of his family before he stepped into eternity. God took his pain and rewrote his story. God wants to do the same with your story.

My Aunt Brenda is closer to God today than she was when Jesse was alive.

My mom is actively involved in her church, pursuing the Lord unlike when my grandpa was alive.

God wants to redeem your pain. I can't say that enough. Your story might look different than my Aunt Brenda's, my mom's, and Job's, but your story matters to God just as much as anyone else's.

I want to encourage you before you move on to the next chapter to take some time to be with Jesus. Get alone with your Bible, journal, pen, and coffee (if you need it like me) and tell him about your pain. I know, you might be thinking, "Aaron, he already knows, so why should I tell him?" Many times, we have not because we ask not. Ask God to rewrite your pain. Ask God to take your story that's full of pain right now and turn it into something beautiful—something extraordinary! God sees our pain. He can take it and use it for a purpose greater than we might be able to see. Our faith must become trust...even in our pain!

You must be willing to be with Jesus to let Jesus rewrite your story. He is willing to spend time with you. Are you willing to make the time to be with him? You'll be better because of it. A moment with Jesus is better, is sweeter, than any moment without him and every story is like a New York Times Bestseller when God writes it. Spend time with Jesus today, tomorrow, and everyday hereafter. Jesus is willing to redeem your pain. The question you need to ask yourself now before moving on is:

Are you willing to let go of the pen and let God rewrite?

CHAPTER 3

WHAT'S BEEN DONE TO YOU

PART 1

I've been rejected many times in my life. There are times when I've allowed rejection to define who I was and what I was able to do. From my rejection, I've experienced the ugliness of being hurt, betrayed, and having felt like I was abandoned. What's been done to you? It could be any number of horrible, wrong, cruel things. We're going to look at rejection—because chances are that's something that's happened to you once, twice, or maybe on multiple occasions—and some other things like betrayal, hurt, and abandonment. Maybe you were rejected, hurt or abandoned by your mom or dad, because they chose their career over you. And now because they've missed most of your football games, recitals, etcetera you feel rejected. Maybe it was a teacher or a coach who rejected or hurt you, because they told you that you weren't smart enough or talented enough. Perhaps a boy or a girl rejected you because they decided that you weren't good looking enough. The reasons could be endless. Someone once told me that rejection is something everyone has or will face, and if anyone says they've never been rejected it's probably because they're too self-absorbed to even notice! I've certainly noticed rejection in my own life. Have you? If we're honest, we've all been rejected, betrayed in some way, hurt in some way, or abandoned in some way.

Allow me to share with you a moment in my life where I allowed rejection to hold me captive for more than a decade. The pain of being emotionally hurt can be a byproduct of rejection, and so can the feelings of being betrayed and abandoned. Oftentimes rejection becomes a problem when we take the bait that declares itself as gospel truth, when in reality it's a lie clothed to imitate truth! I took the bait and as a result rejection held me in a prison for many, many years. And the crazy thing about rejection is that it always hurts the one being rejected more than the one doing the rejecting. It's a lot like unforgiveness. If you harbor unforgiveness it will hurt you. Learning to forgive releases *you* from its dreadful tentacles. And the same is true of rejection. Forgiving those who have rejected you renders rejection powerless to control you. I only wish I would have learned this much sooner in life.

I want to be transparent with you in this book, because truth shared with transparency has much more depth and meaning than truth shared with no personal story attached to it. Story matters. Our lives are stories being written every day. Your story could greatly impact someone else's story for eternity. Jesus told stories to illustrate spiritual truths. That's why you'll find many different types of stories all throughout this book. Stories of rejection—especially personal ones—can be extremely hard to tell. I write this with much grace and dependency upon the Lord to say the right words with the hope of not causing any dissension. My heart is to bring glory to God while telling people truth. Sometimes truth is hard to hear—and write!

I was young—probably not much older than five or six years old (maybe younger). My older brother was going camping with some family members (who will remain unknown for privacy) and I wanted to go so badly. But they told me that they would take me another time, because the two of us would be too much to handle (and rightfully so because my brother and I fought often as do most siblings). Before I had the chance to go camping *another time*, my parents moved my brother and me a thousand miles south to Florida. I left Ohio with a root of rejection planted deep within me, but it didn't surface until I was much older. It took me years to realize that what they said *wasn't* them rejecting me, but that's what the enemy of our souls does. He will take the words of others, twist them, make us feel offended, and turn them into rejection.

You might be thinking: That wasn't that personal of a story. It doesn't sound like that big of a deal. To me it was a very big deal, because as a kid and later as a teenager those words constantly gave me ill feelings toward those family members. Because of a lie, I unknowingly embraced rejection. I've since let it go, realizing it's a lie from the enemy. Forgiveness renders rejection powerless. I have forgiven them long ago, because I realized how the enemy twisted their words and all I heard as a young kid was "rejection." Has something similar happened to you?

We must learn to replace lies with truth. You can't be *in Christ* and *rejected* at the same time because Ephesians 1:11 (NIV) tells us, "In him [*Jesus*] we were also chosen." Jesus hasn't rejected you. He's chosen you! That truth can cancel out feelings of rejection, betrayal, hurt, and abandonment. Of course, it might take time but *in Christ* it can happen! I'm obviously speaking under the assumption you're a believer.

Rejection has many faces. The story of Joseph is one of rejection. It's also a story of how God can rewrite a story of rejection into one that has an impact on thousands of lives! Maybe what's been done to you isn't necessarily rejection. Maybe you were betrayed, you were hurt, or maybe you were abandoned as a young kid. Either way, we can all learn from Joseph's story and take what's been done to him and how he reacted to show that better stories can be written if we only let go of the pen and let God create!

Joseph: An Amazing Story of Grace and Redemption

When you allow God to redeem your story and what's been done to you, you'll be able to live the life you were destined to live. You were created with purpose for a purpose. God has a plan for your life. Each one of us has a story to tell. Each one of us are telling a story—some good, some bad. When God redeems the story a collision of grace, love, and forgiveness occurs that has the power to not only change the trajectory of your life but influence the lives of others to tell better stories.

Joseph's story is a beautiful picture of God's grace and redeeming love changing the life of not just one man, but the lives of thousands of men, women, and children. Of course, no one knew that while certain events in his life were unfolding—such as being betrayed by his own brothers and being tossed into prison for many, many years.

Sometimes we don't see the full picture while the story is being written. Joseph didn't see the ending where his suffering would lead to the saving of so many lives, but he did trust the one who was writing: God!

Joseph was a man with Christ-like characteristics living hundreds of years before the birth of Christ himself. The beauty of Jesus being fully God is he was just as present in the life of Joseph as he was when he walked this earth and as he is today. The Bible makes it clear in Hebrews 13:8 that "Jesus Christ is the same yesterday and today and forever."

You can take Jesus at his word. How do I know this? Well, he did exactly what he said he would do. That tomb is empty! He is alive! And you and I can trust that he is coming back. There are religions in the world where the god they serve is one you can't take at their word. Buddha and Muhammed are still in the grave. Their graves are not empty, because they were mere men. Jesus was fully God, yet fully man. This book isn't a debate about why Jesus is the only way to heaven or why you can take him at his word. I'm simply saying you can trust Jesus. When you collide with the grace of God and are engulfed in his redeeming love you will be changed. His love is radical. It changes you. For me, that's enough evidence to validate the words of Christ. I say all that to make this point: If we can trust what Jesus has to say, we can trust him to write a better story for our lives!

When I collided with the radical love of Jesus my life was wrecked, changed, and given a purpose greater than myself. I believe Joseph truly loved God. From when Joseph was just seventeen years old in Genesis 37, to the day of his death at one hundred and ten years old in Genesis 50, he exemplified God's grace and redemptive love toward others—even those who had wronged him, those who had rejected him, betrayed him, hurt him, and abandoned him. He didn't let what was done to him destroy him. Instead, he trusted God and God used what was done to him for the benefit of thousands.

The story of Joseph is an amazing story of grace and redemption!

Your story can be an amazing story of grace and redemption too!

But before we look more at Joseph, I want to share with you about how words can have a powerful impact on someone. Joseph encountered the power of words in his own life, such as when Potiphar's wife lied about him.[21] Words can make you feel rejected, betrayed, hurt, and abandoned almost as much as anything physical! Words can impact us negatively and positively—depending on what's said of course.

The church I'm on staff with has a women's breakfast every other month. There was a time when my wife was asked to speak at one of the breakfasts. She knew right away God wanted her to share, because he basically gave her everything he wanted her to say within a few hours. Long story short, she went, shared about how God constantly creates and doesn't recreate, and afterwards called me feeling defeated. Why? Because the enemy of our souls was telling her that she didn't do a good job. Comparison had reared its ugly head and the enemy was celebrating because of how defeated she felt.

I did what any godly, loving husband would do.

---

21 See Genesis 39:11–15.

I bought her a year's worth of gerbera daisies—just kidding, I didn't do that. Not a bad idea though, right?

What I did do was love her through it. I told her words of affirmation and encouragement. They helped, but what really confirmed for her that she did well in what the Lord told her to share was what a woman from our church told her later that morning during prayer time.

Side note: One of the things I love about my church—More 2 Life Ministries—is that there is a culture of prayer. Prayer should never be our last reaction, but instead our first response. Every Sunday morning after our time of worshipping the Lord and before the sermon, we have an extended time of prayer. We pray corporately, individually, for needs, for whatever the Holy Spirit prompts us to pray for and about. God has spoken a lot during our prayer time. It's not because we're doing something particularly "holy." It's simply because we are seeking the heart of the Father. Many have come to Jesus during this time of extended prayer! Prayer is important!

The devil loves to whisper lies. Whenever I go to speak somewhere, I hear them often.

You are unqualified.

You can't speak.

You're not as good as so-and-so...

It'd be a lie if I said I never entertained them.

Let's be honest... we all do at times.

Sarah was feeling the weight of the devil's lies. I know the feeling. I'm sure Joseph was too when he was thrown into prison after Potiphar's wife lied about him. When we entertain those lies even for a moment, they can be absolutely destructive to us spiritually and emotionally.

Within a few hours, while praying at church, one of the women who was at the breakfast shared with Sarah how what she'd said spoke directly to her. That it was for her. That she needed to hear exactly what Sarah had shared. When you walk in obedience and do and say exactly what God prompts you to, nothing the enemy does can deter you. Embrace your confidence in Christ, because when you do you will be an unstoppable force and nothing in hell can keep you from doing and saying all that God has purposed for you to do and say. Sarah might have been hurt by the lies of the enemy, but she chose to dwell on who she was in Christ. Nothing the enemy does or says to you can take away who you are in Christ!

What Sarah shared that morning was what I wrote about briefly in the introduction: "One of the coolest things about God is that he doesn't *recreate*. He creates. He doesn't recycle what was bad in order to make something good." My wife significantly influenced me while writing this book. I've learned a lot from her about the beauty of God's grace to rewrite any story. Thankful for her!

God created hope and confidence within Sarah when the enemy wanted to plant lies of discouragement. I'm proud to call her my bride! She inspires me daily to press into Christ and heed his voice above all others.

One time after I had finished preaching at youth, I was standing in the front of the youth room as we wrapped up the night with more worship, and I was feeling the same way Sarah had felt. *Defeated*. I felt like I had done a horrible job at speaking. But then a student came up to me and told me that what I had shared was exactly what he needed to hear. Instantly, words of encouragement replaced the lies from the devil.

So, what's been done to you? Was it something someone said or something someone did? God wants to rewrite whatever it was. He wants to create hope and encouragement within you.

In Christ "we are more than conquerors through him who loved us."[22] You can conquer what's been said to you or about you or what's been done to you by learning to fully embrace what God says about you:

> You are a child of God.[23]
> You are a saint.[24]
> You have been justified.[25]
> You are chosen.[26]
> You are redeemed.[27]

I could go on and on. God says much about our worth and his love for us in his Word. You have much intrinsic value in God's eyes. Your story has meaning. It can be redeemed! The one who fashioned the stars and the planets and put the earth into orbit can rewrite words that have been said to you or situations or circumstances. He's

---

22 Romans 8:37 (NIV).
23 See John 1:12.
24 See Ephesians 1:1.
25 See Romans 5:1.
26 See Ephesians 1:4.
27 See Ephesians 1:7.

more than able to create newness within you despite what's been done to you!

The question is: Will you allow him?

CHAPTER 4

WHAT'S BEEN DONE TO YOU

PART 2

On April 4th, 1945, "the diaries of Admiral Wilhelm Canaris, head of the Abwehr,[28] were discovered, and in a rage upon reading them, Hitler ordered that the Abwehr conspirators be destroyed. Bonhoeffer was led away just as he concluded his final Sunday service and asked an English prisoner, Payne Best, to remember him to Bishop George Bell of Chichester if he should ever reach his home: 'This is the end—for me the beginning of life.'"[29] Bonhoeffer was dealt unfair treatment and eventually was killed at Flossenbürg concentration camp on April 9th, 1945 at the young age of 39. What Hitler and the Nazi regime did to people like Bonhoeffer and millions of others was cruel, unfair, wrong, and inhumane. Sometimes what's been done to us is unspeakable. And

---

28 The Abwehr was a German intelligence organization from 1921 to 1944. The term *Abwehr* (German for "defense") was used as a concession to Allied demands that Germany's post-World War I intelligence activities be for "defensive" purposes only. After February 4, 1938, its name in title was Foreign Affairs/Defense Office of the Armed Forces High Command (*"Amt Ausland/Abwehr im Oberkommando der Wehrmacht"* in German). For more detailed information, read more at http://www.jewishvirtuallibrary.org/the-abwehr.
29 Wikipedia, s.v. "Dietrich Bonhoeffer," last modified October 1, 2019, https://en.wikipedia.org/wiki/Dietrich_Bonhoeffer.

sometimes that involves a lot of regret, pain, guilt, and shame. You can bet people like Dietrich Bonhoeffer,[30] or even Stephen, who was the first person martyred for the Christian faith (see Acts 7:54–60), didn't want such horrible treatment. But what happened was beyond their ability to control and they chose to trust God and give him glory regardless.

Maybe you've been horribly mistreated. I've met people who were abused growing up by a parent or another family member, and I've met people who were abandoned by their parents. So many people I know and don't know have been hurt in ways I could never imagine. Maybe you have. Maybe you know someone who has been. Here's the thing: God wants to redeem what's been done to us. God took what happened to Bonhoeffer and Stephen to speak into countless lives over the years. He wants to use your story too, because no story is beyond the ability for grace and redemption to rewrite. Your story could show someone Jesus and as a result their story is redeemed too. You never know the impact your story can have!

What's been done to you doesn't define you. Your identity is not found in what's been done to you. It's found in Christ. Ephesians

---

30 Bonhoeffer had written *The Cost of Discipleship* (1937), a call to more faithful and radical obedience to Christ and a severe rebuke of comfortable Christianity: "Cheap grace is preaching forgiveness without requiring repentance, baptism without church discipline, Communion without confession. ... Cheap grace is grace without discipleship, grace without the cross, grace without Jesus Christ, living and incarnate." During this time, Bonhoeffer was teaching pastors in an underground seminary, *Finkenwalde* (the government had banned him from teaching openly). But after the seminary was discovered and closed, the Confessing Church became increasingly reluctant to speak out against Hitler, and moral opposition proved increasingly ineffective, so Bonhoeffer began to change his strategy. To this point he had been a pacifist, and he had tried to oppose the Nazis through religious action and moral persuasion. For more details on Bonhoeffer, visit: http://www.christianitytoday.com/history/people/martyrs/dietrich-bonhoeffer.html.

1:7 (ESV) says, "In him we have redemption through his blood, the forgiveness of our trespasses, according to the riches of his grace." In Christ, you are redeemed—you are a new creation who has been bought by the blood spilled at Calvary!

This book is about challenging you to surrender your old story—*to let go of your regrets, guilt, and shame* and let God rewrite your story.

Maybe that means letting God rewrite what's been done to you.

Let's turn to Joseph for a moment.

Joseph was deeply hurt. Any normal human being would be if they were rejected, abandoned and betrayed by their own brothers! Let's look at Genesis 37:18–28 (NIV) for a moment:

> [18] But they saw him in the distance, and before he reached them, they plotted to kill him. [19] "Here comes that dreamer!" they said to each other. [20] "Come now, let's kill him and throw him into one of these cisterns and say that a ferocious animal devoured him. Then we'll see what comes of his dreams."
>
> [21] When Reuben heard this, he tried to rescue him from their hands. "Let's not take his life," he said. [22] "Don't shed any blood. Throw him into this cistern here in the wilderness, but don't lay a hand on him." Reuben said this to rescue him from them and take him back to his father.
>
> [23] So when Joseph came to his brothers, they

stripped him of his robe—the ornate robe he was wearing— ²⁴ and they took him and threw him into the cistern. The cistern was empty; there was no water in it. ²⁵ As they sat down to eat their meal, they looked up and saw a caravan of Ishmaelites coming from Gilead. Their camels were loaded with spices, balm and myrrh, and they were on their way to take them down to Egypt.

²⁶ Judah said to his brothers, "What will we gain if we kill our brother and cover up his blood? ²⁷ Come, let's sell him to the Ishmaelites and not lay our hands on him; after all, he is our brother, our own flesh and blood." His brothers agreed.

²⁸ So when the Midianite merchants came by, his brothers pulled Joseph up out of the cistern and sold him for twenty shekels of silver to the Ishmaelites, who took him to Egypt.

I can't imagine the feelings Joseph had when he was being led away by the Midianite merchants. This is merely conjecture, but it's likely Joseph thought being sold was just as bad as if they had killed him. Either way, he was dead to his brothers! Often—because the enemy thrives on this—we equate rejection as someone wanting nothing to do with us as if we didn't exist. It wouldn't be hard for me to believe that's how Joseph must have felt!

Have you ever been rejected, abandoned, hurt or betrayed by a sibling? Another family member or even a close friend? Think about it for a moment. Here in Okeechobee, where I live, there is a place called Real Life Children's Ranch. It's a place for children who are oftentimes removed from their home due to their parent's inability to care for them. Many times, it is due to drug- and alcohol-related reasons. I imagine Joseph must have felt how some of those children have felt. Rejected. Abandoned. Betrayed. Hurt. Joseph was fully human like you and me. An imperfect person infected with the cancerous disease called sin. I'd bet you a million bucks (if I had it) that Joseph had some pretty strong emotions toward his siblings! I'm sure many of the children at the Ranch do toward their parents! Perhaps you do too toward someone close to you. Know this: You're not alone!

When I was in Washington D.C. in 2017, one of the places I was most excited about seeing was Ford's Theatre and the Peterson House. If you've never been, it should be on your bucket list. Personally, I believe everyone should make a pilgrimage to Washington D.C. at least once in their lives. The city is so full of history; and if you're anything like me, then you likely find history absolutely fascinating. My oldest son will be four years old in October 2019 and I am already planning to take him to Washington D.C. in the future! I want him to not only read about the city in history class—I want him to experience it first-hand—because that changes everything!

On day two of our trip we visited Ford's Theatre and the Peterson House. We got our tickets and waited for the 10 o'clock tour to start. When we went into the museum at Ford's Theatre I was surprised that the very gun used by John Wilkes Booth to kill Abraham Lincoln was on display. I learned a lot about the Booth family on this trip and after, because after visiting Washington D.C. I wanted to know more! That's part of being a history buff, I guess.

John Wilkes Booth was born on May 10, 1838 to "the prominent 19th-century Booth theatrical family from Maryland and, by the 1860s, was a well-known actor. He was also a Confederate sympathizer, vehement in his denunciation of Lincoln, and strongly opposed to the abolition of slavery in the United States."[31]

On April 14, 1865, just after 10:00 p.m., Booth shot Lincoln while he was watching a performance of the play *Our American Cousin* at Washington, D.C.'s Ford Theater. Directly after the shooting, Booth leaped onto the stage and yelled, "*Sic semper tyrannis!* (Thus always to tyrants!) The South is avenged!" Booth next jumped off the stage, breaking his leg in the process, but managed to make it to his getaway horse before anyone in the shocked crowd could stop him.[32]

President Lincoln died the following day across the street at the Peterson House. For me it's almost hard to believe an actor was able to pull off something as big as assassinating the President of the United States of America. Booth came from a prominent theatrical family—a family, I'm sure, that found it hard to rebuild their reputation following the assassination. Obviously I can't speak for them, but I'm almost certain their "prominence" took a bullet as well because of what the young John Wilkes Booth did. Even if what's

---

31 Biography, "John Wilkes Booth," last updated April 16, 2019, http://www.biography.com/people/john-wilkes-booth-9219681.

32 Wikipedia, s.v. "John Wilkes Booth," last modified September 14, 2019, https://en.wikipedia.org/wiki/John_Wilkes_Booth.

been done to you has wrecked or damaged your reputation, it's still not something God can't rewrite and use to help someone else.

I know what's been done to you might pale in comparison to what Booth did to not only Lincoln but his family's reputation.

So why do I even bring up John Wilkes Booth?

Sometimes what's been done to you is beyond your control.

What was done to Joseph in Genesis 37:18–28 was beyond his control.

You can't control people. You can't always control your circumstances or situations either. Booth's family couldn't control the actions John would take in murdering the 16th President of the United States of America. Joseph couldn't control the actions of his brothers when they rejected, abandoned, hurt, and betrayed him like they did.

It's How You Respond

Joseph was dealt several cards that were beyond his control.

1. He was sold by his brothers. (Genesis 37:27–36)
2. He was lied about by Potiphar's wife. (Genesis 39:11–18)
3. He was thrown into prison. (Genesis 39:19–20)
4. He was forgotten by the Cupbearer and left in prison. (Genesis 40:23)

One thing after another happened to Joseph. Ever felt like everything in life was against you? I guarantee Joseph felt like that!

Joseph knew what it felt like to be rejected, betrayed, hurt, and abandoned! I can't say that enough because it's true. I wrestled for a long time whether or not to include the story I am about to share. For one reason: I don't want to paint a bad picture of anyone involved. I am big on honoring people, especially people in any position of authority! Do you want God to honor you? Then honor those whom he has placed in positions of authority over you!

> "Let every person be subject to the governing authorities. For there is no authority except from God, and those that exist have been instituted by God."[33]

❖

I first sensed God calling me to be a pastor when I was sitting in the parking lot of a Walgreens. I asked Sarah (we were dating at the time), "How do you know if you're supposed to be a pastor?" She encouraged me to talk to our pastor about it and so I did. For a while I wrestled with leaving and going to seminary, but Acts 4:13 (ESV)[34] kept coming to the forefront of my mind. Schooling didn't define my calling. If God calls you, it's not because of what school you went to or what degree you have or will get. Now please understand that I am not at all advocating that seminary is bad or that you shouldn't go. I'm simply saying that your calling isn't based on if you go to seminary or not. God calls and equips—my life is evidence of that.

Long story short, I ended up not going to seminary. I married

---

33 Romans 13:1 (ESV).
34 "Now when they saw the boldness of Peter and John, and perceived that they were uneducated, common men, they were astonished. And they recognized that they had been with Jesus."

Sarah, and decided to continue working at the retail store I was employed at. I wanted to go into ministry and I wanted people to know I had been with Jesus. The solution seemed pretty obvious, but even then, the decision took time. I wanted to know for sure that I was doing what God wanted me to do. Within a month or so after our wedding God opened the door for me to step into bi-vocational youth ministry. The church where I was offered the youth pastor position was another local church nearby, but one that had different views on certain teachings. At first, I wrestled with it but ultimately was able to simply trust that this was where God was leading Sarah and me. After a month of seeking the Lord, praying, talking to my wife, and praying some more the Lord told me clear as day to go! This was God calling me. I knew I needed to answer that call so I accepted the offer to be the youth pastor, but eventually something happened that was beyond my control.

No doubt Joseph loved his brothers. Even though they seemed like complete jerks I'm sure he still cared about them. And vice versa—despite what they did to their younger brother! I don't think it was that they didn't love Joseph. I think it had to do more with the fact they were jealous of Joseph! What happened to us a few years after accepting the youth pastor position offer wasn't personal. But that didn't stop what happened from hurting us nor from it being beyond our control.

I had no idea that stepping into this role would end up hurting us (and thankfully God has since healed us). My wife and I faithfully served for a few years before everything changed—abruptly, I might add. The church we were at had a falling out—the details wouldn't do any good to share other than it was all beyond our control—and as a result my relationship with my pastor at the time changed. It was almost as if I had been cut off—abandoned and betrayed to some degree. I don't think this was on purpose. Did it hurt? Absolutely! Am I angry? No. Have I forgiven him? Completely. Regardless of the "why", it was beyond my control when our close relationship came to a sudden end.

To this day, I have no hard feelings toward him. I see him occasionally and love him just the same—and I am sure he does too. We have moved onto different areas of life—but what happened to me was still hard nonetheless! Losing that close friendship with someone who had invested so much into me hurt. It would be a lie to say it didn't.

Has something like that happened to you?

Anything beyond your control?

A close relationship suddenly end?

Even when a relationship comes to an end, it can be God working. I've found this to be true. We might have parted ways, but I still love my pastor at the time dearly because of how much he invested in me, encouraged me, and helped me learn to heed the Lord's voice. But our stories were going in two different directions. Some stories God pens intertwine for many, many years. Some only for short seasons. Either way, the "founder and perfecter of our faith"[35] knows what's best!

It was beyond my wife's control when the enemy bombarded her with all that negativity after speaking at the women's breakfast.

---

35 Hebrews 12:2 (ESV).

It was beyond Stephen's control when the people agreed to stone him to death, making him the first martyr of the Christian faith.

It was beyond Joseph's control when his brothers plotted to sell him as a slave.

It was beyond the Booth family's control when John Wilkes Booth decided to assassinate the President of the United States of America.

When my relationship with my pastor at the time was cut off I knew I needed to respond how Joseph responded to his brothers in Genesis 50:15–21 (ESV) after Jacob had died.

> [15]When Joseph's brothers saw that their father was dead, they said, "It may be that Joseph will hate us and pay us back for all the evil that we did to him." [16]So they sent a message to Joseph, saying, "Your father gave this command before he died: [17]'Say to Joseph, "Please forgive the transgression of your brothers and their sin, because they did evil to you."' And now, please forgive the transgression of the servants of the God of your father." Joseph wept when they spoke to him. [18]His brothers also came and fell down before him and said, "Behold, we are your servants." [19]But Joseph said to them, "Do not fear, for am I in the place of God? [20]As for you, you meant evil against me, but God meant it for good, to bring it about that many people should be kept alive, as they are today. [21]So do not fear; I will provide for you and your little ones." Thus he comforted them and spoke kindly to them.

I always want to speak kindly about my pastor at the time, about anyone in any position of authority, about people in general. Speaking words of negativity only breeds destruction and creates dishonor.

God doesn't honor dishonoring people!

I want to honor God by honoring others! And you should too!

How Joseph responded is how we should respond to what's been done to us. I know that's easier said than done! I also know what's been done to you might be physical, verbal, emotional, or maybe a combination of all three! It might be worse than anything I have ever been through. I'm not downplaying your pain nor am I suggesting what's been done to you can easily be overcome. But there is hope! The Bible says in Romans 15:13 (ESV), "May the God of hope fill you with all joy and peace in believing, so that by the power of the Holy Spirit you may abound in hope." God is the source of our hope! God *is* our hope! Despite what's been done to you, the more time you spend with God, the more hope will overflow from you "by the power of the Holy Spirit."

Intertwined within Joseph's response was an unwavering trust in God. Though what happened to him was horrible, God's purpose for it was much greater than Joseph himself! What his brothers meant for evil God intended for good—to help countless others in a desperate time! Maybe what's been done to you is in preparation to someday help someone else going through what you're going through or have been through.

Whenever something beyond my control happens I often find

myself chewing on Romans 8:28 (ESV): "And we know that for those who love God all things work together for good, for those who are called according to his purpose."

God has given us free will. And sometimes free will leads to bad decisions, and bad decisions lead to problems and situations that are many times beyond our control. A prime example is Joseph's brothers choosing to sell their younger brother into slavery. Remember, you can't control other people. You can only control what choices you make. I know God is bigger than any problem, circumstance, or situation I may face. I know God is bigger than what's been done to me! God is big enough to use what the devil and people intended for evil to be intended for something good—something greater than ourselves! Joseph believed that. You can see that he believed it by how he responded to his brothers:

> "'So do not fear; I will provide for you and your little ones.' Thus he comforted them and spoke kindly to them" (Genesis 50:21, ESV).

Would Joseph speak kindly after everything he went through if he didn't believe God could use what happened for not only his good but the good of countless others? I don't think so. The same applies to your story! I know it might be hard to see any good if you're in a particularly hard place. But no situation or circumstance disproves the reality that God loves you and is for you. Our faith must become trust. Joseph didn't waiver in his faith in God. Even when bad things happen to you that doesn't change the truth that God is still good and can use what's been done to you for good.

Joseph responded with much grace!

God responded to our sin with much grace by choosing to leave the splendor and glory of heaven and die on a rugged cross for our sins!

Do you think God would have honored Joseph if he didn't show grace toward his brothers? Even when someone wrongs you we must remember they are in need of forgiveness just like you and me! Again, I'm not trying to downplay what's been done to you. But we do need to understand, even when it's hard to do, that grace isn't limited to just you. Joseph had an understanding of grace. For God to rewrite what's been done to you, grace must first be received, but also extended toward others who have wronged you.

Whatever has happened in your story so far, God can use it for your good! Whenever we go through a trial it's never just about us. It's so you can also pour into someone else who might be facing what you faced. God is more intelligent than a crafty, cunning serpent who caused man to fall. God knew Genesis 3 would happen. God knew Joseph's brothers would sell him. God knew my son would be in the NICU when he was born. God knew that what happened to you would happen. But he is more than able to rewrite what happened to create a much better story—a story filled with much hope, amazing grace, and redeeming love.

An entire book could be written based on the life of Joseph. I could only include a small portion in this book and that still doesn't cover half of what we could learn by zooming in on his life. To recap: Joseph was rejected and betrayed by his own family, falsely convicted and thrown into prison, yet all the while unwavering in his faith. He's an example to follow in how we should respond to what's been done to us. In my opinion, Joseph is someone who models what it looks like to be Christ-like. And the crazy thing about that—Joseph lived long before Jesus physically walked the earth! That goes to show you how even during Joseph's day, God could be known! And he can be known today too! Your story can be rewritten, and written within a grander story, greater than any you could tell yourself.

God redeemed Joseph's story and exalted him to the position as the second-most-powerful man in Egypt (see Genesis 41:27–45). God rewrote what was done to him and used it to save countless lives. God wants to take what's been done to us and use it to help others.

Let God rewrite!

And respond like Joseph!

CHAPTER 5

DESIRES

PART 1

Christmastime somehow manages to be incredibly over-commercialized, yet also the most wonderful time of the year. I love Christmas! I'm not opposed to Black Friday or the fact that Walmart has Christmas trees up in their stores before Thanksgiving. As a kid, one of the things I loved about this time of the year was making my Christmas list for Santa. It had everything that I desired to unwrap on Christmas morning. Some of the items on my Santa list over the years included: A golf cart, a toy Mechagodzilla, a guitar, a basketball, a cassette tape of a country singer whose name I can't seem to remember (probably because it was in the mid-90's), a Bible, and socks (yes, as you get older it's funny how your "Christmas list" changes).

What are some things you have desired for Christmas? I wish I could say I always got everything I included on my Christmas list. It's pretty obvious that we all have desires. The Bible says in Psalm 37:4 (ESV), "Delight yourself in the Lord, and he will give you the desires of your heart." But before you start thinking God is going to give you that new car or the winning lottery ticket simply because you desire it, it's imperative you understand that our desires are not always lined up with God's desires. Let me explain.

The prerequisite for taking "delight in the Lord" is knowing the Lord. I'm going to assume if you're reading this you've got that part covered. You can't know the heart or desires of someone you don't know. Knowing God opens that door to knowing his desires for your life.

When I was high school I desired to be a number of different things from an author, to a meteorologist, to a computer programmer. When I graduated from Okeechobee High School in June of 2008, my desires changed yet again from a Crime Scene Investigator, to a journalist, to an English teacher. That's just to name a few. I switched majors a lot! I'm now a pastor still living in Okeechobee and I wouldn't trade it for anything! It wasn't until I began to follow Jesus that my life changed and with that life change came new desires—God-honoring desires, I might add!

A Rememberable Spot

I have what I like to call a "rememberable spot" that I look back at and visit quite often. It's a reminder of when and where God birthed a life-changing desire within my heart. I mentioned it in the previous chapter. I was in my car in the Walgreens parking lot in Okeechobee, Florida when a certain thought—or desire, I should say—shot across my mind. I can't remember the exact date except that it was between the fall of 2010 and the spring of 2011 (it's one of those moments I wish I had written down in a journal). Regardless of the specific date, that parking lot is a reminder, a remembrable spot, because it's when I first heard God impress this question within my spirit: *How do you know if you're supposed to be a pastor?*

I believe one of the ways God speaks to us is in the form of questions. It's those questions that lead to certain decisions or opportunities or adventures that would otherwise never happen if the question was never asked. That question in the Walgreens parking lot led me to seeking counsel with my pastor at the time, to helping with the youth, to marrying Sarah, to stepping into bi-vocational youth ministry for two years, to eventually taking a leap of faith of going into full-time ministry. But it all started with a simple question—the birthing of a new desire—in that Walgreens parking lot.

What's your remembrable spot? Do you have a moment in time or place where you can pinpoint God birthing a new desire or desires within you?

Maybe you're wondering, why even bring up having such a spot? Well, like anything, mankind has a tendency to mess things up. And oftentimes that's even without the devil getting his hands dirty. Here's the reality: I believe there are many people—many who will read this book and especially this chapter—who once had such a spot, a God-birthed desire—that they've neglected, forgotten, abused, or otherwise never pursued because of bad decisions. To sum it up, their sin hindered their God-birthed desire from ever sprouting and growing into all God purposed and planned.

But there's good news!

If that's you or someone you know, God's grace is more than

enough to wipe away any regret, mistake, and shame and allow that desire to sprout once again. We serve the God of many second chances. I can't speak for God and say for certain what your second chance will look like, but I can promise you if you confess your sin and return to him, he'll forgive you. And God's forgiveness is the first step toward your desires being redeemed so that they honor and bring him glory!

So, you've messed up. Or maybe you've simply never really given much thought about your desires or the desires God has placed deep within your spirit. I will be upfront with you: when we honor God, he'll honor those God-birthed desires within you! You can't expect God to honor selfishness, but you can expect God to honor those God-birthed desires that are selfless and will bring him much glory!

Your Greatest Desire

Let me ask you a question: How much do you *desire* Christ?

Let me reword it this way: Do you desire miracles more than the miracle giver? Do you desire answered prayers more than the one who can answer them? Do you desire physical healing more than the Great Physician? Do you desire eternal life more than the lifer-giver himself? What's your greatest desire?

God wants to redeem your desires. Redeemed desires honor God and bring him glory. Redeemed desires magnify the name of Jesus. Redeemed desires care more about God's reputation than any person's reputation. Here's the thing: Maybe your life has been caught up in one desire after the next that was sinful in nature and not God honoring whatsoever. It could be sexual desire outside

God's design. It could be caring more about money and your career than God or your family. It could any number of things. I might not have listed them directly but God knows. But know this: The Lord is willing to redeem them! But you must take a step of faith, repent, trust in Jesus, and know that God will never turn away a repentant heart.

The greatest desire in your heart will tell you who or what your life worships. I truly believe that. If your greatest desire is the Lord Jesus Christ, then your life is a worship song to the King of kings. If it's your career, your spouse, your hobby, an addiction, or anything else, then that desire is an idol, a false god, and will leave you empty, hopeless, and dead. Let's look at a man named Polycarp for a moment.

> Polycarp was a personal disciple of the Apostle John. As an old man, he was the bishop of the Church at Smyrna in Asia Minor (present-day Turkey). Persecution against the Christians broke out there and believers were being fed to the wild beasts in the arena. The crowd began to call for the Christians' leader Polycarp. So the authorities sent out a search party to bring him in. They tortured two slave boys to reveal where Polycarp was being hidden.
>
> Polycarp's captors came in to arrest him as if he were a murderer. "They came in like a posse, fully armed as if they were arresting a dangerous criminal." And then what happened next is nothing short of amazing. Polycarp didn't resist, fight or try

to flee. No, he did the exact opposite! "Polycarp welcomed his captors as if they were friends, talked with them and ordered that food and drink be served to them. Then Polycarp made one request: one hour to pray before they took him away. The officers overhearing his prayers (that went on for two hours) began to have second thoughts. What were they doing arresting an old man like this?"

Polycarp was threatened to be burned alive. I love his response to those wishing to take his life. It showed his heart and his love for the Lord Jesus!

His response was: "You threaten fire that burns for an hour and is over. But the judgment on the ungodly is forever."

The fire was prepared. Polycarp lifted his eyes to heaven and prayed: "Father, I bless you that you have deemed me worthy of this day and hour, that I might take a portion of the martyrs in the cup of Christ. . . Among these may I today be welcome before thy face as a rich and acceptable sacrifice."[36]

Reading this, I think it's easy to guess what Polycarp's greatest desire was. *It was Jesus.* Your greatest desire will rise to the surface when under intense pressure. Don't let that be the only time you realize what it is. Ask yourself right now. *What is my desire? My greatest*

---

36 Christianity.com, "Who Was Polycarp?" April 28, 2010, https://www.christianity.com/church/church-history/timeline/1-300/polycarp-11629601.html.

desire? If it's anything other than Jesus Christ, know this: If you're still alive there's still time to change that!

In February of 2018 the famed evangelist Billy Graham passed away and changed his address to heaven. What a life he lived! It was a life that reflected the love of God through a man who needed Jesus as much as you and I do. He desired for all people to know Jesus, but his greatest desire was always Jesus himself. When Jesus is your greatest desire, everything else you do will be with that desire in mind!

"Billy Graham was named by Americans as 'One of the Ten Most Admired Men in the World,' a record-breaking 59 times with the Gallup poll. He was known through the years as not only a world-renowned evangelist, but as a kind, non-judgmental, accepting, and humorous soul.

His message is timeless, powerful, and relevant for today. The phrase, 'the Bible says,' resounds throughout his sermons, and the truth he preached for years still transcends all barriers of denominational differences, age, nationality, and culture. It has stood the test of time and generations, pointing millions to Christ. The Reverend Billy Graham preached God's Word with conviction and passion for over 60 years."[37]

Read one of Billy Graham's books, watch one of his sermons, or talk to someone who knew him and you'll see a man whose greatest

37 Debbie McDaniel, Crosswalk, "40 Courageous Quotes from Evangelist Billy Graham," accessed October 7, 2019, https://www.crosswalk.com/faith/spiritual-life/inspiring-quotes/40-courageous-quotes-from-evangelist-billy-graham.html

desire was Jesus, and overflowing from that desire was a love for people the world doesn't see often.

I share about Billy Graham and Polycarp to let you know that these men lived out their greatest desire, and that you can too. You can put to death those sinful desires, repent of those desires that have taken you down a path of shame, and have full assurance that Jesus Christ can redeem your desires for his glory. My own life is a perfect example of just that.

Prior to giving my life to Christ, my life revolved around me, what I wanted, when I wanted it. God was never my first and greatest desire. My greatest desire was whatever my flesh desired, and as a young man that usually involved the girl I was dating. I don't need to go in detail for you to understand that. Here's the beauty of the gospel message: It changes those desires, because the Bible is very clear that when someone is born again in Jesus Christ they are "a new creation. The old has passed away; behold, the new has come."[38] Praise God for new life—and new desires—in Jesus Christ!

I've had a desire to write since I was twelve years old. Before coming to Christ, I wrote three books—one in high school and two in college. They didn't bring glory to God, and neither would I recommend anyone read them. After finding new life in Jesus in October of 2009, I hit a major roadblock in my writing. I wrote one more book not long after I got saved called "Streets of Gold" that you can probably still find on Amazon (though if you read it please read it with much grace). I wrote it for the wrong reasons. I wanted to write another book to get my name out there—I desired

---

38 2 Corinthians 5:17 (ESV).

selfish gain—and I was under a contract I didn't want to pay to get out of. Over the years I still desired to write, but could never finish what I started. It wasn't until I gave up writing *what I wanted* and began writing what God called me to write that I was finally able to achieve a desire I've had since I was twelve years old. In the spring of 2017 I began writing this book you're reading—a book God placed in my heart to write, a book that I truly believe was a God-birthed desire!

God redeemed my desires once I learned to relinquish control, delight in only him, and strive first for his kingdom alone. I believe it's possible to give your life to Jesus and then, sometimes without us realizing it, desires that are not God ordained often creep back into our lives. That's when we need to "seek first the kingdom of God"[39] and allow God to birth new desires in us that will honor him.

You are not too far gone for God to redeem your desires.

You have not done too much wrong.

You have not sinned too much where God's grace can't find you.

You don't have too much shame because of past sinful desires that God can't forgive you, heal you, and birth new desires within you.

God can redeem your story and write new desires that can change your life.

---

39 Matthew 6:33 (ESV).

CHAPTER 6

DESIRES

PART 2

In my opinion, the Apostle Paul is the perfect example of how God can redeem desires—how God can redeem the story. Your life is a story unfolding. Each day is a new chapter, a new beginning. Up until Paul's story unfolded on the Damascus road, he was known to be a persecutor of Christians. John Piper writes on *Desiring God*, "Paul's public life, before and after his conversion to Christ, was known by hundreds, probably thousands. His transformation, from murderer to lover, was widely known and undeniable. He is not claiming a private conversion experience. He is stating a public fact. His own explanation was that he had seen the risen Jesus and received forgiveness and a mission."[40]

Paul writes in Galatians 1:13; 23–24 (CSB):

> "For you have heard about my former way of life in Judaism: I intensely persecuted God's church and tried to destroy it . . . They simply kept hearing:

---

40 Desiring God, John Piper, "Why I Love the Apostle Paul," published October 18, 2016, https://www.desiringgod.org/articles/why-i-love-the-apostle-paul#1-a-massive-change-came-into-paul-s-life-through-his-experience-on-the-damascus-road-and-turned-him-from-being-a-killer-of-christians-into-being-a-lover-of-christ-and-his-people

"He who formerly persecuted us now preaches the faith he once tried to destroy." And they glorified God because of me.

Prior to encountering Jesus on the Damascus road, it's easy to assume Paul's desire was to kill Christians—to stop the spread of the message of Christ at all costs. Before you picked up this book, maybe your desire was for sex outside of marriage, to get drunk every weekend, to gossip regularly… I don't know what it is or was for you, but I do want you to know that if you're reading this then chances are God is wanting you to know that he wants to redeem those desires, replace them, and use you to spread the message of the gospel to the world you are a part of everyday!

Let's take a look at Paul's desires before the event on the Damascus road. The first verse in Acts 8 says that "Saul [*later known as Paul*] approved of his [*Stephen's*] execution."[41] In the previous chapter, verses 57–58, we get a picture of Saul's desire:

> [57] They yelled at the top of their voices, covered their ears, and together rushed against him. [58] They dragged him out of the city and began to stone him. And the witnesses laid their garments at the feet of a young man named Saul. (CSB)

The Apostle Paul, the one who would eventually write much of the New Testament, the one who would be a vessel God used to reach thousands with the hope found only in Jesus Christ, was at one time a murderer of the church! Paul's story is amazing, because it shows that if God can redeem Paul's desires he can redeem our

---

41 Acts 8:1 (ESV), with author clarification.

desires today! Granted, most of our desires pale in comparison to what Paul did before coming to Jesus. Nonetheless, they can still be just as wicked in God's eyes.

Later, Paul writes in Romans 13:13–14 (ESV), "Let us walk properly as in the daytime, not in orgies and drunkenness, not in sexual immorality and sensuality, not in quarreling and jealousy. But put on the Lord Jesus Christ, and make no provision for the flesh, to gratify its desires." When we delight ourselves in the Lord, it's putting on the Lord Jesus Christ and realizing your old life and all those desires have now been nailed to the cross. For some, sexual impurity is the desire that pulls; for others it's the quarreling and jealousy; for others it's the carousing and drunkenness; but no matter what the desire was, you can put on the Lord Jesus Christ today and know without a shadow of a doubt that God will redeem your desires. He can redeem them in such a way that even if years have gone by, you can begin afresh with hope for the future.

Paul encountered Jesus and his desires were redeemed.

When you encounter Jesus, your desires can be redeemed. Sometimes we tend to believe Satan's lie that certain desires are okay, when in reality they are in opposition to God and his kingdom.

Maybe you've been gratifying the desires of the flesh. God can redeem your story.

Maybe those desires have kept you from truly growing in your walk with the Lord. God can change that.

Maybe those sinful desires have blinded you to the reality of truly knowing the risen Jesus. Today can be the day of your salvation (or if you know the Lord already, the beginning of a new chapter in your story!).

Paul's life is a testimony of a life redeemed in many ways. One of those ways is that his desires began to change the moment he encountered Jesus on the Damascus road. Maybe reading this chapter can be your moment.

Your greatest desire is usually what you seek first above anything else. For Paul it was once killing Christians, and later it became the very One (Jesus) he once opposed.

For me it was once a toxic relationship in high school.

It was once wanting to fit in with the "cool people".

It was once many, many other things.

What is it for you? Or, better yet, what *was* it?

What Are You Seeking First?

Matthew 6:33 (ESV) says, "But seek first the kingdom of God and his righteousness, and all these things will be added to you."

What "things" is this verse referring to? The previous two verses shed some light on this:

> Therefore do not be anxious, saying, "What shall we eat?" or "What shall we drink?" or "What shall we wear?" For the Gentiles seek after all these things, and your heavenly Father knows that you need them all (Matthew 6:31-32 ESV).

We often seek worldly care or things of this world first before seeking God. Usually our desires dictate what we seek most. God knows the things you need, such as food and clothing, but when our focus shifts to dwell only on what we need or what we fear or what we want, it keeps us from seeking God first. He knows those desires you have that hinder you from first seeking his kingdom. Desires can become an idol and so can food, clothing, a career or a relationship. The first thing to help you successfully run the race called life and finish well is ensuring you don't take your eyes off of the one who sustains you while you run and who waits for you at the finish line. *That's Jesus.* That's why Jesus must be our greatest desire! Jesus can provide for all your needs and can satisfy all your wants (and desires). The problem is oftentimes we don't seek him first; and so we easily get caught up in the things of this world and that's usually when we find ourselves wondering why we aren't hearing the voice of God! It's because we aren't seeking him first!

We mustn't neglect intimacy with God for the things of this world. Neglecting to seek first God's kingdom will result in growing weary from worldly cares, such as fear, worry, unforgiveness, and anger, to name a few. You'll be dragged down by things such as those and they'll hinder you from running well. If you want to run the race with the Lord's hand on you like it was on Elijah,[42] then it begins with prioritizing God above all else!

Grab a piece of paper. Write down the first thing that pops into

---

42 1 Kings 18:45–46 (ESV): "And in a little while the heavens grew black with clouds and wind, and there was a great rain. And Ahab rode and went to Jezreel. And the hand of the Lord was on Elijah, and he gathered up his garment and ran before Ahab to the entrance of Jezreel."

your head after reading the following question: *What do you think most about?*

The answer to that question says a lot about your priorities. If I'm honest, sometimes I think a lot more about everything else in my life instead of seeking God first above everything. Maybe you do too.

❖

Facebook has officially hit 2 billion monthly users, solidifying the company's position as the largest, most influential social network in the world.[43] Every one of these users see the "*What's on your mind?*" question when they log on. It's really another way of asking the same question I just asked you. Only Facebook allows you to see the answer for anyone you are friends with or follow. Facebook is a digital window into what you think about most. For thousands of people it's the perfect selfie, or what's for dinner, or the latest breaking news story of the day. If we're honest with each other, what we think about most can actually be a lot of different things considering how fast we process information thanks to social media giants like Facebook, Instagram, and Twitter. We live in a "I want it my way" and "I'm offended" society where someone could be seeking multiple things instead of seeking first the kingdom of God. Whether it's wanting something their way or something they're offended over, these things draw them away from seeking God first. And if you are seeking God first, selfishness has to die and any offenses must go. The current state of our society tells me many aren't dying to self

---

43 Forbes, Kathleen Chaykowski, "Mark Zuckerberg: 2 Billion Users Means Facebook's 'Responsibility Is Expanding,'" published June 27, 2017, https://www.forbes.com/sites/kathleenchaykowski/2017/06/27/facebook-officially-hits-2-billion-users/#2558f8653708.

and are holding onto offenses as if they are valuable like gold; when in reality, it's weighing them down in the race called life.

Instead of seeking what's on your friend's minds on Facebook every morning, seek first the kingdom of God.

Instead of seeking the perfect selfie everywhere you go, seek first the kingdom of God.

Instead of always worrying only about what you're going to wear, seek first the kingdom of God.

Instead of_____ (what is it for you?), seek first the kingdom of God.

I'm not suggesting you can't browse Facebook, take selfies, plan your outfits or anything like that. If we do these things but never place seeking God first and most important, we're not running the race well.

What are you seeking more than anything else right now?

Is it money?

Is it fame?

Is it a relationship?

Is it a new job?

If we aren't careful the enemy of our souls will make sure the things we are seeking are placed before seeking first the kingdom of God. And that's a dangerous place to be.

As Christians, we should desire seeking first God's kingdom

more than anything else. There's nothing else this world can offer that can fill the void within each of us that only Jesus can!

Your desires can be redeemed. I can't say that enough. After all, this book is all about how God can redeem!

Desires of Opportunity

When we are totally sold out for Jesus and he has redeemed our desires, supernaturally cool things can happen! Opportunities, for example, can pop up out of the blue. I often pray the prayer of Jabez[44] believing God can expand my influence, and He's done that many, many times! I can remember one moment in particular where I prayed for God to give me more opportunities to speak—side note: a desire I have is to preach and tell people about Jesus—and that desire was answered unexpectedly. God has done that often!

In the beginning of 2018, I was praying for what I knew to be a God-birthed desire—opportunities to preach and tell people about Jesus. I always pray for opportunities, because I believe it's a God-given desire that was redeemed from a selfish life full of selfish desires. It's cool how God can take even the selfish desires we have and redeem them and birth new ones in us that bring him much glory. I was once a super shy, quiet kid who now loves to speak, who loves to tell people about Jesus, and can stand in front of a crowd of any size to preach without any fear. That's what happens when God redeems! He also empowers! God can redeem your desires also

---

44 1 Chronicles 4:10: "Jabez called upon the God of Israel, saying, 'Oh that you would bless me and enlarge my border, and that your hand might be with me, and that you would keep me from harm so that it might not bring me pain!' And God granted what he asked." (ESV)

by giving you new ones too. If he did it for me—and for countless others—he can do it for you too!

It was mid-January and we had just started worship at youth group. I don't normally answer my phone once the service begins. But something in my spirit told me I should answer the phone when my good friend Jay was calling. I stepped outside and took the call. To my surprise, Jay called to invite me to be the guest speaker at an event called Winter Splash in Asheboro, North Carolina on February 3rd, 2018. I immediately went back to the desire God had given me to pray for opportunities to speak. He was answering that prayer—that desire! Jay told me that he didn't think about it being a Wednesday night at 6:30pm, which was the time of our weekly youth service. He had told me that God had laid me on his heart and if I answered the phone he would take that as a yes that he heard from God correctly.

When God redeems our desires and births new ones in us, amazing things can happen! For me, it's opportunities to live out a desire he birthed within me, which is preaching. Desires of opportunity are a direct result of God redeeming my desires. I truly believe that. This short story is just one example of many where God has answered my prayer for doors to be opened to preach. And no matter how many times God surprises me, I'm still amazed at the fact that he loves me enough to redeem what was once full of such selfishness and wickedness. I still have a heart that can be sinful, but thank God for his amazing grace and the mercy he lavishes to redeem what was wicked for his greater purposes!

I don't know where you're at or what you're going through, but those desires you have that are not God honoring, that go against what God's Word teaches on how a Christian should live, can be redeemed. Your desires are not too far gone for the Creator of all things to rewrite them with new passion and purpose. I'll end this chapter with a quote from my favorite author, Mark Batterson. He writes in his book *Whisper*: "Some desires are sinful, no doubt. And those sinful desires must be crucified. But God also wants to resurrect them, sanctify them, intensify them, and leverage them for His purposes."[45]

---

45 Mark Batterson, *Whisper: How to Hear the Voice of God* (New York: Multnomah, 2017).

CHAPTER 7

WILL YOU ANSWER THE CALL?

O ne of the things that's repeated often throughout this book is that God can redeem.

Repeating a truth can be beneficial.

The Bible is repetitious on a lot of things.

"The use of repetition in the Bible usually emphasizes the importance of a person, theme, or event. This makes sense for the Gospels because the story of Jesus' earthly ministry and mission is the most important event in the history of the world. The presence of four distinct accounts of Jesus' life emphasizes His importance.

"The repetition of the Gospels offers greater credibility. In the ancient world, legal testimonies were considered valid if they could be substantiated by at least two or three witnesses (see Deuteronomy 19:15). By having four separate accounts written by four distinct witnesses, the Bible offers a highly reliable portrait of who Jesus was and what He did on our behalf.

"The use of repetition in the Gospels allowed the biblical authors to approach Jesus' story from different angles and perspectives."[46] I hope and pray you see by now (if you hadn't before) that God can and wants to redeem your story. I've repeated that thought many times in this book praying it sinks in. If you're anything like me, I need things repeated often for them to take root.

Before I wrap up this short book, I want to take a moment to look at how God can and desires to redeem the words we speak or write. After all, words are a big part of our everyday life whether we are talking or writing. Isn't it great to know the Lord can redeem even the careless words we have spoken? For me, that's a huge relief!

Our Words

I couldn't have been much older than five or six years old. I was lying in my bed and I remember clearly uttering the hateful words to God, "I'll kill you, God!" Years later—after I gave my life to Christ—I asked my pastor at the time about what I had spoken years earlier and if God can forgive me for saying something so mean—something so *evil*. He reminded me of a truth that I want to share in this chapter. And that truth is this: No matter the words we have spoken, God can still redeem our stories! *The words we speak can be redeemed!* As a new believer, knowing that brought me huge relief. Because what I had spoken as a child was, quite honestly, from the pit of hell! Even today, as I've entered into my third decade of life, knowing this truth gives me great peace because God is more gracious than any of us deserve!

---

46 ThoughtCo, Sam O'Neal, "The Importance of Repetition in the Bible," last updated June 25, 2019, https://www.thoughtco.com/the-importance-of-repetition-in-the-bible-363290.

I've said some pretty stupid things over the years. There are words, phrases and sentences I regret and there are moments when anger got the best of me and what I spoke was belligerent and dumb. As a result of speaking in such a way, usually nothing good follows. But when my words are uplifting and sweet to the soul, I find joy, peace… fulfillment.

Proverbs 18: 21 (ESV) says, "Death and life are in the power of the tongue, and those who love it will eat its fruits."

Your words matter.

What you say matters.

What you write (or type) matters.

It has the power to build someone up or tear them down. And that someone can be yourself!

Words Cut Deep

When I was in the first grade I got bullied. A lot. I remember one day I was waiting for my mom to pick me up. It was the end of the school year and I had found out I was going to be held back. Somehow word got out to some of my peers. I don't recall this, but my mom validates that this did actually happen. After one of my peers made fun of me for having to repeat the first grade I apparently snapped back, "Well, I'm going to go through first grade again and I'll be smarter than you!" Laugh if you want. Not much logic behind what I said, *but* deep down the words spoken to me cut deep. Obviously they hurt if I still remember them twenty plus years later.

Words, whether you've written or spoken them, have the ability to cut deep.

But no wound caused by words is too big for God to heal.

And no word you've written or spoken is beyond the reach of God's grace.

I thought it fitting to end this book with this idea that God can redeem the words we have written or spoken.

"On average a person speaks at least 7,000 words a day, with many speaking much more than that. Think about what that means to you. Those 7,000 words (at least) you speak each day are your imprint on the world. They dictate how people perceive you—and largely define you."[47]

And that's not including how many words you write!

I can only imagine how the words Peter spoke on the night of Jesus' arrest and betrayal must have cut deep into Jesus' flesh. Yes, he was God but he was also fully man. And I'm sure those words of denial cut deep.

> "[54]Then they seized him and led him away, bring-
> ing him into the high priest's house, and Peter
> was following at a distance. [55]And when they had
> kindled a fire in the middle of the courtyard and
> sat down together, Peter sat down among them.
> [56]Then a servant girl, seeing him as he sat in the

---

47 LinkedIn, Paul Petrone, "You Speak (at Least) 7,000 Words a Day. Here's How to Make Them Count," accessed October 7, 2019, https://learning.linkedin.com/blog/advancing-your-career/you-speak--at-least--7-000-words-a-day--here-s-how-to-make-them-.

light and looking closely at him, said, "This man also was with him." ⁵⁷But he denied it, saying, "Woman, I do not know him." ⁵⁸And a little later someone else saw him and said, "You also are one of them." But Peter said, "Man, I am not." ⁵⁹And after an interval of about an hour still another insisted, saying, "Certainly this man also was with him, for he too is a Galilean." ⁶⁰But Peter said, "Man, I do not know what you are talking about." And immediately, while he was still speaking, the rooster crowed. ⁶¹And the Lord turned and looked at Peter. And Peter remembered the saying of the Lord, how he had said to him, "Before the rooster crows today, you will deny me three times." ⁶²And he went out and wept bitterly" (Luke 22:54-62, ESV).

Even though just hours prior Jesus told Peter he would do it, Peter still was broken over the words he spoke. Verse 62 says that he "went out and wept bitterly." That, to me, shows a man who is completely broken over what he has done.

There have been moments in my life where I wanted to "weep bitterly" over my choice of words, whether written or spoken. Maybe that's you too.

I've got great news for you: Like Peter, God wants to redeem those words.

That's great, right?

You might be thinking, Aaron, you don't know the things I've said about myself, about others and to others. It's horrible. It's unforgivable.

Peter spent three years watching Jesus heal the sick, give sight to the blind, and raise the dead. And he blatantly denied knowing Jesus. Yet, God's grace and redeeming love reached Peter still.

Maybe you've said some pretty horrendous things.

Maybe you've posted on social media some hateful, racist remarks; and even though you deleted them, you still feel the guilt of having written them.

Words we speak or write are most often an overflow of what's in our hearts. When God redeems our stories, he has the power to renew our hearts. When God changes our hearts, that's when our words begin to change.

Just like how Jesus restored Peter, and he went on to preach his very first sermon in Acts chapter 2 where thousands came to Jesus, Jesus can restore you. He can rewrite your story with better words. He can speak hope, love, grace and peace over you. I can't make you. God can't make you. You must make the choice to let God redeem and rewrite.

❖

God wants to redeem all people… no matter who they are.

God wants to redeem your pain.

God wants to rewrite what's been done to you.

God wants to redeem your selfish, sinful desires.

God wants to rewrite your life story, because your story isn't over.

It doesn't matter who you are, where you are or what you've done. God can—and desires to—redeem your story. The only question that needs answering is:

Will you answer the call to let God rewrite your story?

CLOSING WORDS

Thank you for reading this short book. Writing it has been quite the journey. This book has actually been in the works for more than two years. And the topics I've included are ones I've faced and other people I know have faced over the years.

You might think of something I should have included in this book or a chapter I should have written. That's okay! I'm sure after publishing this book, I'll think of some things too! Maybe you have some thoughts on some things God can redeem that I didn't mention, or maybe you want to share what God has already rewritten in your life.

You can reach out to me in a few different ways:

X	@AaronJosephHall
Instagram	@theAaronHall89
Facebook	@pastoraaronhall
Website	HallMedia.org

I'd love to connect with you! God bless!

—Aaron

AARON HALL

Aaron is the husband to Sarah and dad to four amazing boys. He's the Lead Pastor at Jubilee City Church in Daphne, Alabama, where he and his family live. He was born in Cincinnati, Ohio but has lived most of his life in South Florida before moving to plant Jubilee City. Learn more about him online at HallMedia.org and the church at JubileeCity.church.